BBC micro:bit Recipes

Learn Programming with Microsoft MakeCode Blocks

Pradeeka Seneviratne

Apress®

BBC micro:bit Recipes: Learn Programming with Microsoft MakeCode Blocks

Pradeeka Seneviratne
Udumulla, Mulleriyawa, Sri Lanka

ISBN-13 (pbk): 978-1-4842-4912-3   ISBN-13 (electronic): 978-1-4842-4913-0
https://doi.org/10.1007/978-1-4842-4913-0

Copyright © 2019 by Pradeeka Seneviratne

Managing Director, Apress Media LLC: Welmoed Spahr
Acquisitions Editor: Natalie Pao
Development Editor: James Markham
Coordinating Editor: Jessica Vakili

Cover image designed by Freepik (www.freepik.com)

Distributed to the book trade worldwide by Springer Science+Business Media New York, 233 Spring Street, 6th Floor, New York, NY 10013. Phone 1-800-SPRINGER, fax (201) 348-4505, e-mail orders-ny@springer-sbm.com, or visit www.springeronline.com. Apress Media, LLC is a California LLC and the sole member (owner) is Springer Science + Business Media Finance Inc (SSBM Finance Inc). SSBM Finance Inc is a **Delaware** corporation.

For information on translations, please e-mail rights@apress.com, or visit http://www.apress.com/rights-permissions.

Apress titles may be purchased in bulk for academic, corporate, or promotional use. eBook versions and licenses are also available for most titles. For more information, reference our Print and eBook Bulk Sales web page at http://www.apress.com/bulk-sales.

Any source code or other supplementary material referenced by the author in this book is available to readers on GitHub via the book's product page, located at www.apress.com/978-1-4842-4912-3. For more detailed information, please visit http://www.apress.com/source-code.

Printed on acid-free paper

Table of Contents

About the Author

Pradeeka Seneviratne is a software engineer with over 10 years of experience in computer programming and systems design. He is an expert in the development of Arduino and Raspberry Pi-based embedded systems. Currently he is a full-time embedded software engineer working with embedded systems and highly scalable technologies. Previously, Pradeeka worked as a software engineer for several IT infrastructure and technology servicing companies.

Pradeeka is an author of many books: *Building Arduino PLCs* (Apress, 2017), *Internet of Things with Arduino Blueprints* (Packt, 2015), *Raspberry Pi 3 Projects for Java Programmers* (Packt, 2017), *Beginning BBC micro:bit* (Apress, 2018), and *Hands-on Internet of Things with Blynk* (Packt, 2018).

CHAPTER 1

MakeCode Setup Fundamentals

In this chapter, you will learn how to set up and work with MakeCode for micro:bit, which is one of the most popular development tools to create micro:bit applications. Like many other software frameworks, MakeCode for micro:bit has a wide array of extensions (packages) to choose from.

You will also learn how to get started with the MakeCode for micro:bit and build some basic applications for micro:bit.

1-1. Starting Microsoft MakeCode for BBC micro:bit

Problem

You want to start the Microsoft MakeCode for BBC micro:bit to build a micro:bit application using **Blocks**.

Solution

- Using your web browser, go to `https://www.microsoft.com/en-us/makecode` to open the **MakeCode landing page**.

© Pradeeka Seneviratne 2019

P. Seneviratne, *BBC micro:bit Recipes*, https://doi.org/10.1007/978-1-4842-4913-0_1

- In the **Hands on computing education section**, click **Start coding with micro:bit** (**Figure 1-1**).

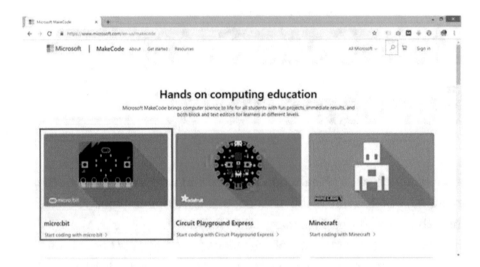

Figure 1-1. *Landing page for Microsoft MakeCode*

You can go directly to makecode.microbit.org.

- In the **MakeCode for micro:bit home page**, in the **My Projects** section, click on the **New Project** (**Figure 1-2**).

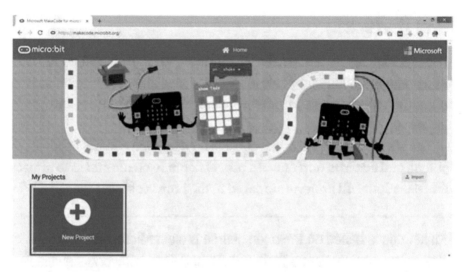

Figure 1-2. *Landing page of the MakeCode for micro:bit*

- The **MakeCode editor for micro:bit** will start on your browser (**Figure 1-3**).

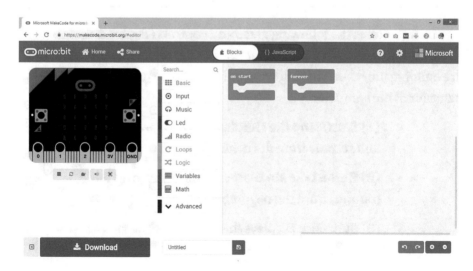

Figure 1-3. *MakeCode editor for BBC micro:bit*

How It Works

Microsoft **MakeCode** is a web-based online editor that allows you to build programs using snappable blocks. It is also known as a graphical programming language and supports all modern web browsers and platforms.

The **MakeCode** website uses cookies for analytics, personalized content, and ads. You don't need a user account to create and save projects with MakeCode. All projects are saved in the browser's local cache.

MakeCode is based on the open source project Microsoft Programming Experience Toolkit (PXT), and its framework is available at `https://github.com/Microsoft/pxt`.

MakeCode provides environments such as BBC micro:bit, Adafruit Circuit Playground Express, Minecraft, LEGO MINDSTROMS Education EV3, Cue, Chibi Chip, and Grove Zero.

The editor has the following areas and controls (**Figure 1-4**).

Simulator - Provides the output without the real hardware while you are building the code. The following buttons can be used to control the behavior of the simulator.

- **(1) Start/Stop the simulator**: Stops the program and restarts from the beginning.

- **(2) Restart the simulator**: Restarts the program (output) from the beginning.

- **(3) Slow-Mo**: Displays the output in slow motion.

- - **(4) Mute audio**: Mutes audio when you're working with music and speech.

  - **(5) Launch in full screen**: Shows the simulator in full screen mode.

- **Toolbox** - Provides blocks in categories. Also allows you to search extensions in the toolbox and add more extensions (packages) to the toolbox if available.

- **Coding Area** - The area you use the build the code with **Blocks** and write the code with **JavaScript**.

- **Editor Controls**

  - **Home** - Takes you to the home screen (`https://makecode.microbit.org/`), which shows recent projects and other activities.

  - **Share** - Displays the **Share Project** window that lets you publish your project to the public cloud and embed your project in to a web page with different options.

  - **Blocks or JavaScript** - Allows you to switch the code view from **Blocks** to **JavaScript**, or back again. Press one of the **view buttons** at the top and center of the window.

  - **Help** - Shows a menu with help options such as support, reference, blocks, JavaScript, hardware, and where to buy.

  - **More... (gearwheel)** - Allows you to access project settings, adding extensions, deleting the current project, deleting all the projects, choosing a language, and pairing micro:bit for one-click download.

- **Undo and Redo** - Allows you to undo and redo recent changes you make either in Blocks or JavaScript with the **Undo** and **Redo** buttons in the bottom right of the editor window.

- **Zoom In and Zoom Out** - The zoom buttons change the size of the blocks when you're working in the **Blocks** view. When you're working with the code in the **JavaScript** view, the zoom buttons change the size of the text.

- **Save Project** - You can type a name for your project and save it. Type in a name for the project in the text box, and press the **disk icon** to save.

- **Download** - The **Download** button will copy your program to a drive on your computer.

- **Show/Hide the simulator** - The **Show/Hide the simulator** button can be used to show or hide the simulator.

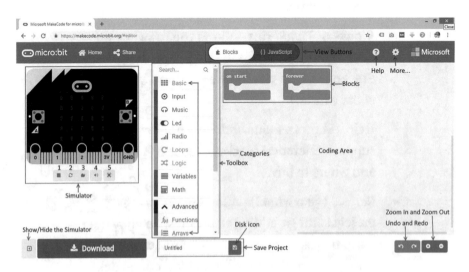

Figure 1-4. *Important areas and controls on the MakeCode editor*

By default, the coding area is focused to the **Blocks** view with **on start** and **forever** blocks.

1-2. Saving a Project to a File

Problem

You want to save your work to a file.

Solution

- In the **project name** box, type in a name for your project and click on the **Disk** icon. The new name of the project is updated in your browser's local cache. Meanwhile, a **hex file** will download to your computer.

- If you click on the **Disk** icon without providing a new name for the project (with the default file name, Untitled), the **Rename your project** modal box (window) will pop up (**Figure 1-5**).

Figure 1-5. *Renaming a project*

- Now type in a name for the project, and click on the
  Save button. The project will save under the new file
  name, and the new name of the project is updated in
  your browser's local cache. Meanwhile, a **hex file** will
  download to your computer (**Figure 1-6**).

Figure 1-6. *Downloading a hex file*

Files you've downloaded are automatically saved in the **Downloads**
folder. You can always move downloads from the Downloads folder to
other places on your computer.

How It Works

With MakeCode, your code will automatically save as you work under the
default project name Untitled. All projects are saved in the browser's local
cache. You can save your project by providing a new file name. If you don't
name your project, it's kept as an 'Untitled' project. You can save your
project to a file or in the cloud (see **Recipe 1-6. Sharing a Project**).

The download location can be configured with your web browser. It
could be a local drive in your computer, a removable drive, or a network
drive.

- If you want to use the default project named **Untitled**,
  just click on the **Save** button in the **Rename your
  project** modal box without providing a new project
  name.

- If you click on the **Save** icon after saving the project under a new project name, any changes you have made will save, and a hex file of the project will download to your computer.

1-3. Downloading a Project

Problem

You want to download a project into your computer as a hex file.

Solution

- Click on the **Download** button in the bottom of the page. A hex file will download to your computer (**Figure 1-7**).

Figure 1-7. *Downloading the hex file*

The downloaded hex file can be found with your browser.

- **Google Chrome**: The downloaded hex file will appear (list) in the **Download Bar** at the bottom of the browser. Click on the **caret (circumflex)** icon and from the shortcut menu, click **show in folder** to open the folder it was saved to using the default file browser on the system. You can also access the downloaded file by clicking on **three dots (⋮)** icon in the top-right corner of the browser

and click **Downloads** from the menu or press **Ctrl+J.**
Then in the **Downloads** page, click **Show in folder** link
to open the folder for the corresponding file.

- **Microsoft Edge**: When asked what to do with this file,
  select **Save** and it will be saved to your **Downloads**
  folder. Selecting Open Folder will allow you to view
  your downloads.

- **Mac Safari**: When you select **Download in Safari**, your
  file will appear under **downloads** in the top right of the
  screen; you can open your downloads folder from here.

How It Works

When you click on the **Download** button, the code is compiled in the
browser and downloaded as a hex file.

Usually the downloaded hex file can be found in the **Downloads** folder
in your computer. The word **microbit** will append to the start of the file
name. As an example, if you have a project named **Hello World**, the name
of the downloaded hex file would be **microbit-Hello-World.hex**.

1-4. Flashing a Hex File to the micro:bit

Problem

You want to flash a downloaded hex file to the micro:bit.

Solution

- Connect the micro:bit to your computer using a micro
  USB cable (use the micro USB port on the top of the
  micro:bit).

- Once it has been mounted, find the micro:bit in the file manager and open it. An example shows if a Windows-based system is used (**Figure 1-8**). Drag and drop the hex file into the open micro:bit window.

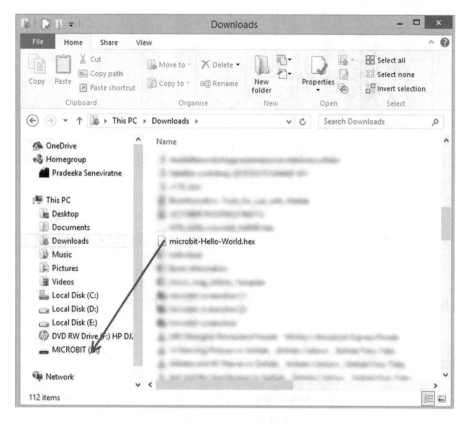

Figure 1-8. *Copying a hex file to the micro:bit drive*

- If you're using Google Chrome browser, you can drag and drop the hex file on the micro:bit drive from the browser's **Download Bar** if available (**Figure 1-9**).

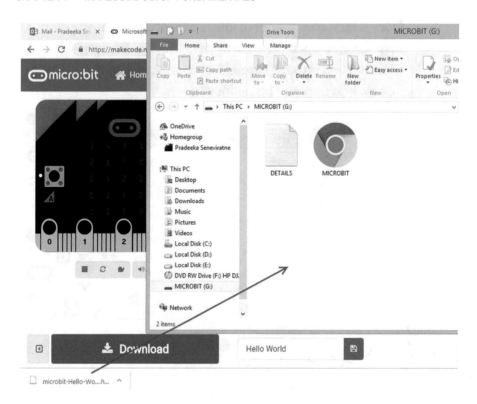

Figure 1-9. *Copying a hex file to the micro:bit drive*

How It Works

The process of transferring a hex file to the micro:bit is called flashing.
The LED on the back of your micro:bit flashes during the transfer. Once
this has completed, the micro:bit will automatically restart and start
executing your code.

1-5. Changing the Download Location to micro:bit Drive with Google Chrome

Problem

You want to download the hex file from the MakeCode directly to the micro:bit drive.

Solution

- On your computer, open **Chrome**.

- At the top right, click **Customize and control Google Chrome** (three-dotted button).

- From the drop-down menu, click **Settings**.

- Scroll down the page and at the bottom, click **Advanced** to expand the page or type **Downloads** in the search bar with the magnifying glass.

- Under the **Downloads** section, click on the **Change** button and select the micro:bit drive (**Figure 1-10**).

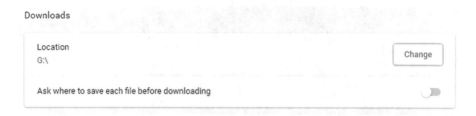

Figure 1-10. *Setting the downloads location*

How It Works

Google Chrome allows you to configure the download location for your files. Changing the default download location to the micro:bit drive allows you to flash the hex file to the micro:bit with a single click.

1-6. Sharing a Project

Problem

You want to share your project.

Solution

- In the **Editor controls**, click on the **Share** button (**Figure 1-11**).

Figure 1-11. *Sharing a project*

- In the **Share Project** window, click on the **Publish project** button (**Figure 1-12**).

Figure 1-12. *Publishing a project*

- In the **Share Project** modal box (window), click on the **Copy** button to copy the address to the clipboard (**Figure 1-13**).

Figure 1-13. *Sharing a project link*

- If you want to embed your project in a website, click on the **Embed** link to expand the **Share Project** modal box (**Figure 1-14**).

Figure 1-14. *Embedding a project in a website*

- The expanded section provides you three options.

    - **Code** - Embeds Blocks or JavaScript of your project
      (**Figure 1-15**).

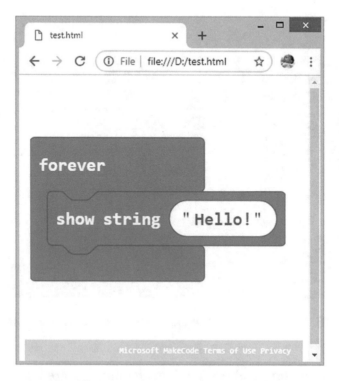

Figure 1-15. *Embedding blocks or JavaScript of the project*

- **Editor** - Embeds the editor with minimal user interface.
  You can jump to the full-featured editor by clicking on
  the **Edit** button in the top-right corner of the embedded
  view (**Figure 1-16**).

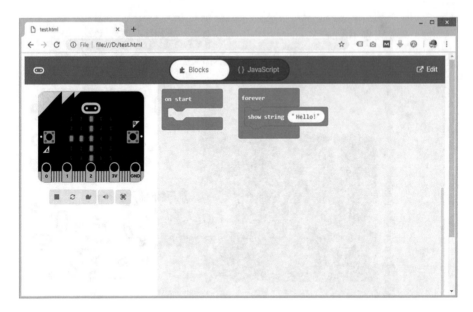

Figure 1-16. *Embedding the MakeCode editor with minimal user interface*

- **Simulator** - Embeds the simulator only (**Figure 1-17**).

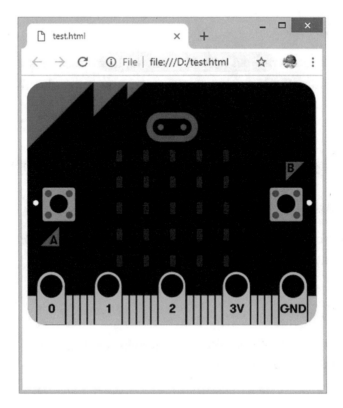

Figure 1-17. *Embedding the micro:bit simulator*

- Click on the large **Copy** button to copy the html code to the clipboard.

- Open a text editor, such as Notepad, and paste the html code into the editor window.

- Save the file with an .html extension. This will allow the system to know it's a html file.

- After saving the file, open it with your web browser by either typing the path in the address bar or dragging and dropping the file into the browser window.

How It Works

When you create a project with MakeCode, it will receive a unique identifier. This identifier is used with when sharing and embedding your code.

1-7. Opening a File from the Computer

Problem

You want to open a micro:bit project on your computer with the MakeCode editor for micro:bit.

Solution

- In the MakeCode editor for micro:bit, click on the **Import** button (**Figure 1-18**).

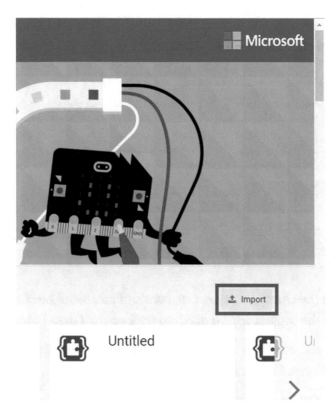

Figure 1-18. *Import button on the MakeCode editor*

- In the **Import** window, click on the **Import File...**
  button (**Figure 1-19**).

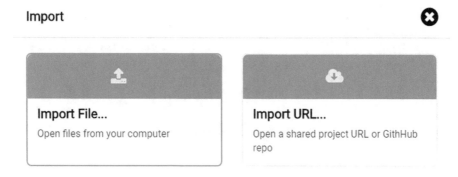

Figure 1-19. *Importing a project from the file*

- In the **Open hex file...** modal box, click on the **Choose File** button (**Figure 1-20**).

Figure 1-20. *Choosing a hex file to open*

- In the **Open** dialog box, browse and locate the hex file of the project you want. Then click on the **Open** button.

- If you want to open a different project, click on the **Choose File** button again.

- In the **Open hex file...** modal box, click on the **Go ahead!** button to open the project (**Figure 1-21**).

Figure 1-21. *Choosing a hex file to open*

- The project will load into the MakeCode editor for micro:bit.

How It Works

micro:bit code files use the .hex file extension. These are normally referred to as 'hex files'.

When MakeCode compiles the code, it compiles it in a format that is compatible with itself and allows it to decompile a MakeCode hex file and display the correct blocks.

Hex files that have been compiled in non-MakeCode environments, such as MicroPython or Mbed, will have a differing format that MakeCode will not be able to understand and display.

1-8. Opening a Shared Project

Problem

You want to open a shared project from a URL or from the GitHub repository.

Solution

- In the MakeCode editor for micro:bit, click on the **import** button.

- In the **Import** modal box (window), click on the **Import URL...** button.

- In the **Open project URL** modal box, paste the URL of the shared project or URL of the GitHub repository.

- Click on the **Go ahead!** button.

- The project will load into the MakeCode editor for micro:bit.

How It Works

Publicly shared micro:bit projects can be accessed using the shared URL or URL provided by the GitHub repository. However, be cautious when using software or following instructions from unknown sources.

1-9. Deleting a Project

Problem

You want to delete a project from the MakeCode.

Solution

- In the **Editor controls**, click on the **More...** button.

- In the drop-down menu, click **Delete Project** (**Figure 1-22**).

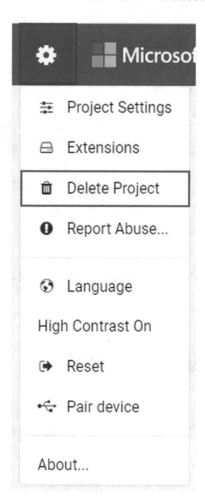

Figure 1-22. *Deleting a project*

- In the delete confirmation modal box (window), click
  on the **Delete** button (**Figure 1-23**).

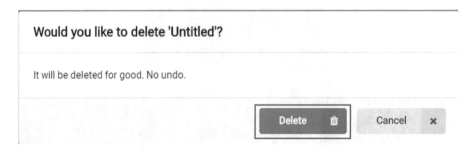

Figure 1-23. *Confirm dialog box for delete a project*

How It Works

The **Delete Project** option will remove your project from the browser's local cache.

1-10. Deleting All Projects

Problem

You want to delete all the projects in your MakeCode editor.

Solution

- In the **Editor controls**, click on the **More...** button.
- In the drop-down menu, click **Reset** (**Figure 1-24**).

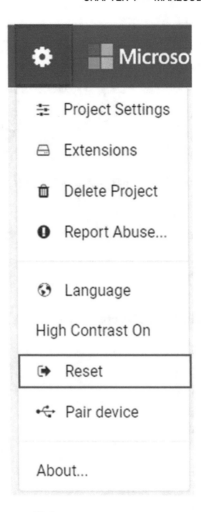

Figure 1-24. *Deleting all the projects*

- In the **delete confirmation** window, click on the **Reset** button (**Figure 1-25**).

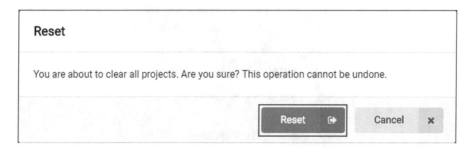

Figure 1-25. *Confirm dialog box for deleting all the projects*

- This will delete all projects from the local storage.

How It Works

The **Reset** option will **remove** all your projects from the browser's local cache.

CHAPTER 2

MakeCode Extended Features

In this chapter you will learn some extended features of MakeCode that allow you to manage extensions (packages) and pare them with your micro:bit for One-Click download using WebUSB.

2-1. Adding an Extension from the Extension Page

Problem

You want to add an extension to the toolbox of the MakeCode editor.

Solution

- In the **Editor controls**, click on the **More...** button.
- In the drop-down menu, click **Extensions** (**Figure 2-1**) or use the **add Extensions** under the **Advanced** tab.

© Pradeeka Seneviratne 2019
P. Seneviratne, *BBC micro:bit Recipes*, https://doi.org/10.1007/978-1-4842-4913-0_2

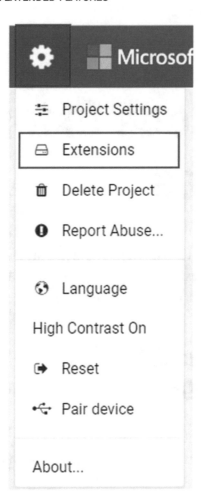

Figure 2-1. *Extensions menu option in the More... menu*

- In the **Extensions** page, click on the extension that you
  want to add to your project (e.g., **Servo**) (**Figure 2-2**).

Figure 2-2. *Extensions page*

- If you can't find the extension that you want to add to your project in the **Extensions** page (e.g., **SparkFun Moto:bit**), type the name of the extension (try typing in what you trying to find, for example, with **time** then type **time** in the search box.) in the **Search or enter project URL...** textbox and click on the **Search** button. The page will show you all the matching extensions based on your search string. Now, click on the correct extension to add to your project (**Figure 2-3**).

Figure 2-3. *Search result for the SparkFun extensions*

- The Blocks and JavaScript definitions for the new
  extension will be automatically loaded in the editor
  and can be found in the **Toolbox** as a **Category**
  (**Figure 2-4**).

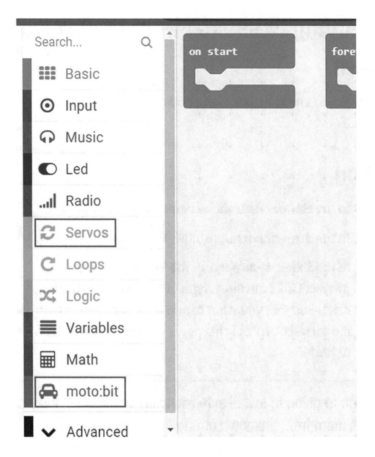

Figure 2-4. *Newly added extensions in the Toolbox*

How It Works

By default, MakeCode displays enough blocks in the toolbox to allow you to create code using the micro:bit out of the box. This toolbox can be extended to allow the micro:bit to use expansions, such as a robot board, and add functionality such as the ability to control NeoPixels or similar.

The Extensions system also ensures that only compatible extensions are installed and will automatically resolve any compatibility issues.

2-2. Adding Extension from the Project URL

Problem

You want to add an extension to the MakeCode editor from the project URL.

Solution

- In the **Editor controls**, click on the **More...** button.

- In the drop-down menu, click **Extensions**.

- In the **Extensions** page, in the **Search or enter project URL...** textbox, type in the project URL of the extension that you want to add (e.g., the project URL of the **4tronix BitBot** is `https://github.com/4tronix/ BitBot`).

When you're going to install extensions on MakeCode, make sure not to install them from unknown or unofficial sources.

- Click on the **bitbot** from the search result (**Figure 2-5**).

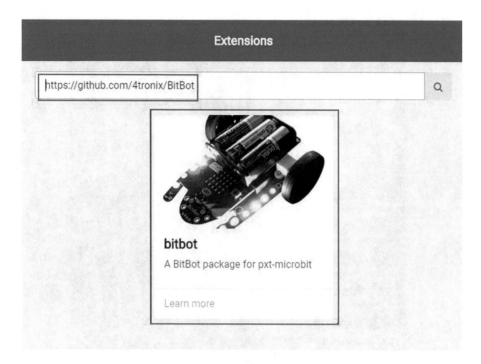

Figure 2-5. *Adding an extension from the GitHub*

- The Blocks and JavaScript definitions for the new
  extension will be automatically loaded in the editor and
  can be found in the **Toolbox** as a **Category** (**Figure 2-6**).

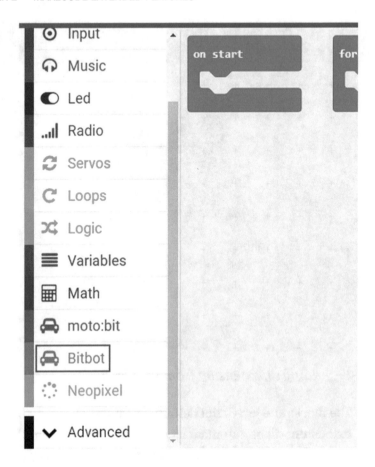

Figure 2-6. *The Bitbot extension*

How It Works

The advanced users have published their own extensions and can be found in the MakeCode for micro:bit documentations page (https://makecode.microbit.org/extensions).

Extensions were previously called Packages in MakeCode.

Here is the list of extensions currently available.

- **Robotics**
- 4tronix BitBot
- SRS BitBot
- Sunfounder Sloth
- UCL Junk Robot
- Kittenbot RobotBit
- inex iBit
- k8 robotics bit
- Gigglebot
- Robobit
- Pi Supply Bit Buggy
- ALS Robot Coo
- ALS Robot CruiseBit
- Hummingbird Bit
- **Gaming**
- Sparkfun Gamer:bit
- **STEM**
- micro:turtle
- NeoPixel
- Sparkfun Moto:bit
- Sparkfun Weather:bit
- Minode Kit

- Grove inventor kit

- WS2812B

- Pimoroni Envirobit

- MakerBit

- **Sensing and Individual Components**

- MAX6675

- Sonar

- Bluetooth Temperature Sensor

- Bluetooth MAX6675

- ssd1306 OLED

- ky040 rotary

- GY521

- PCA9685 LED controller

- Imagimaker Magishield

- gator:light Light sensor

- gator:temp Temperature Sensor

- ALS Robot Electromagnet

- **IoT**

- Pi Supply Lora Node

- **Other**

- File System

- Code Dojo Olney

- File System

- MIDI

- Bluetooth MIDI

- BlockyTalkyBLE

- Katakana

- Muselab WiFi IoT Shield

- LINE BLE beacon

- Pimoroni Scrollbit

- SBRICK

- Pimoroni Automationbit

- Annikken Andee

- ALS Robot Keyboard

2-3. Removing an Extension from the Project

Problem

You want to remove an extension from the project.

Solution

- In the **Editor controls**, click on the **More...** button.

- In the drop-down menu, click **Project Settings**.

- In the **Project Settings** page, click on the **Explorer** menu (left navigation menu) to expand.

- Find the extension that you want to delete and click on the **Delete icon (Figure 2-7)**.

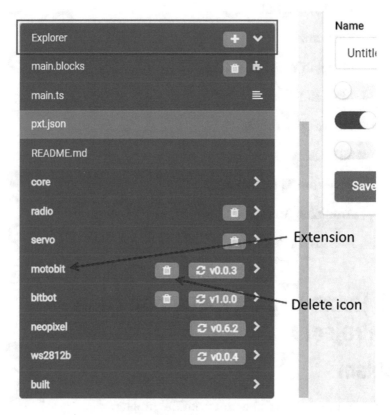

Figure 2-7. *Deleting an extension*

- In the **Remove extension** window, click on the **Remove It** button to confirm the deletion (**Figure 2-8**).

Figure 2-8. *Confirmation dialog box for delete an extension*

How It Works

You can't remove **core extensions** from your project. The delete option is only available for third-party extensions.

2-4. Pairing micro:bit for One-Click Download Using WebUSB

Problem

You want to directly flash a hex file to the micro:bit from the MakeCode editor using **WebUSB**.

Solution

- Before pairing, check the firmware version of your micro:bit (see **How It Works** section).

- Connect the micro:bit to your computer with a USB cable.

- In the **Editor controls**, click on the **More...** button.

- In the drop-down menu, click **Pair device**.

- In the **Pair device for one-click downloads** window, click on the **Pair device** button (**Figure 2-9**).

Figure 2-9. *Pairing device for one-click downloads*

- In the **makecode.microbit.org wants to connect** window, select **BBC micro:bit CMSIS-DAP** or **DAPLink CMSIS-DAP** from the list and click on the **Connect** button (**Figure 2-10**).

Figure 2-10. *Choosing DAPLink CMSIS-DAP*

- Once your micro:bit is paired, MakeCode will use WebUSB to transfer the code without having to drag and drop.

How It Works

WebUSB currently supports the following platforms.

- Chrome 65+ browser for Android
- Chrome OS, Linux
- macOS
- Windows 10

Make sure that your micro:bit is running version **0249** or above of the firmware. You can upgrade your firmware to the latest version by following these steps.

- Go to the **MICROBIT** drive.

- Open the **DETAILS.TXT** file.

- Find the line says the version number of the firmware (**Figure 2-11**).

Figure 2-11. *Finding the micro:bit version number using details. txt file*

- If the version is **0234**, **0241**, or **0243**, you need to update the firmware on your micro:bit. If the version is **0249**, **0250**, or higher, you have the right firmware and are ready to pair your device with the MakeCode.

- Now put your micro:bit into MAINTENANCE Mode. To do this, unplug the USB cable from the micro:bit and then reconnect the USB cable while you hold down the reset button. Once you insert the cable, you can release the reset button. You should now see a MAINTENANCE drive instead of the MICROBIT drive like before. Also, a yellow LED light will stay on next to the reset button.

- Download the latest firmware .hex file from `https://microbit.org/guide/firmware/`.

- Once downloaded, drag and drop that file onto the MAINTENANCE drive.

- The yellow LED will flash while the HEX file is copying to the micro:bit. When the copy finishes, the LED will turn off and the micro:bit resets. The MAINTENANCE drive now changes back to MICROBIT.

- Now open the DETAILS.TXT file to check and see that the firmware version changed to the match the version of the HEX file you copied (**Figure 2-12**).

Figure 2-12. *Content of the DETAILS.txt file*

CHAPTER 3

MakeCode Programming Basics

In this chapter you will learn how to manage blocks in the coding area and about programming basics with simple recipes. These recipes can be used to build more advanced programs later with MakeCode. As an example, the recipe **displaying numbers** can be used to display the results of a formula in a complex program.

3-1. Adding Blocks onto Coding Area

Problem

You want to add blocks onto the coding area from the Toolbox.

Solution

- In the **Toolbox**, click on any **Category** and from the **submenu**, click on the block you want to place on the coding area (**Figure 3-1**).

© Pradeeka Seneviratne 2019
P. Seneviratne, *BBC micro:bit Recipes*, https://doi.org/10.1007/978-1-4842-4913-0_3

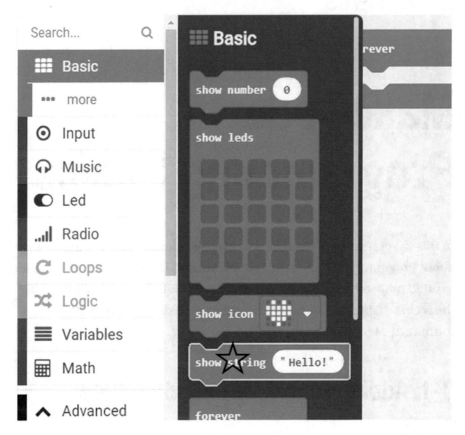

Figure 3-1. *Placing a block on the coding area by clicking on it*

- Otherwise, you can **drag and drop** a block onto the coding area (**Figure 3-2**).

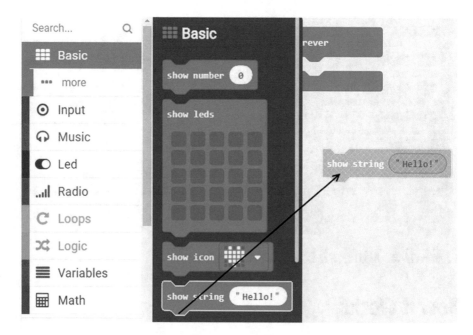

Figure 3-2. *Placing a block on the coding area by drag and drop*

- After placing the block, you can further move it to any place on the coding area by dragging and dropping (**Figure 3-3**).

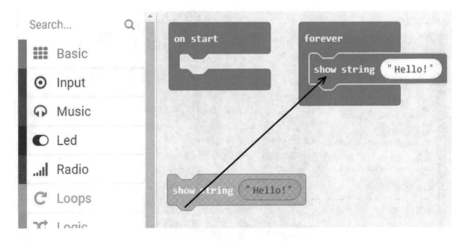

Figure 3-3. *Moving a block on the code area*

How It Works

MakeCode organizes blocks with categories by grouping similar or related blocks together. By default, MakeCode shows the following block categories in the Toolbox:

- Basic

- Input

- Music

- Led

- Radio

- Loops

- Logic

- Variables

- Math

- Functions

- Arrays

- Text

- Game

- Images

- Pins

- Serial

- Control

3-2. Deleting a Block

Problem

You want to delete a block from the coding area.

Solution

Do one of the following:

- In the coding area, click on the block you want to delete and from the keyboard, press the **DELETE** key.

- In the coding area, right-click on the block you want to delete. Then, click **Delete Block** from the shortcut menu (**Figure 3-4**).

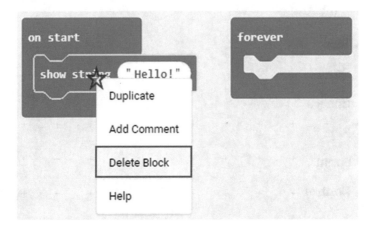

Figure 3-4. *Deleting a block*

- Drag and drop the block into the **Toolbox** (**Figure 3-5**).

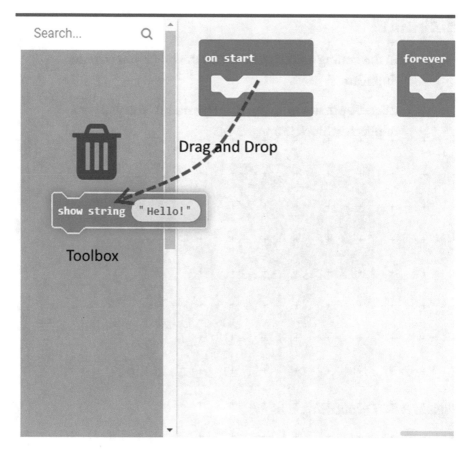

Figure 3-5. *Deleting a block*

How It Works

This will remove the selected block from the coding area. You can undo it by clicking on the **Undo** button in the bottom right of the window.

3-3. Duplicating a Block

Problem

You want to duplicate a block in the coding area.

Solution

- In the coding area, right-click on the block you want to duplicate.

- Click **Duplicate** from the shortcut menu. You will get a duplicated block (**Figure 3-6**).

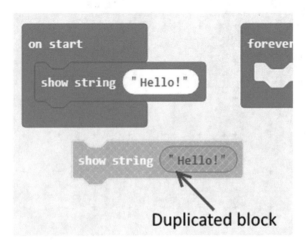

Figure 3-6. *Duplicating a block*

How It Works

This option allows you to quickly duplicate an existing block in the coding area without choosing it again from the Toolbox. Duplicate will create a **clone** of a selected block.

3-4. Adding a Comment

Problem

You want to add a comment to a block.

Solution

- In the **coding** area, ***right-click*** on the block you want to add a comment.

- Click **Add Comment** from the shortcut menu.

- In the comment box, type in a comment for the block.

- Click on the hide icon (arrow head) in the top-left corner of the comment box to hide (**Figure 3-7**).

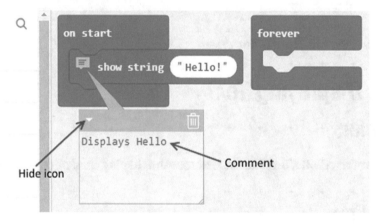

Figure 3-7. *Adding a comment*

How It Works

Comment boxes are useful to add text note to a block to provide explanatory information, usually about the function of the code. These comment blocks are generally ignored by the compiler.

If hidden, you can show the comment box again by clicking on the comment icon in the left side of the block. If you want to delete the comment, just click on the delete icon on the top-right corner of the comment box (**Figure 3-8**).

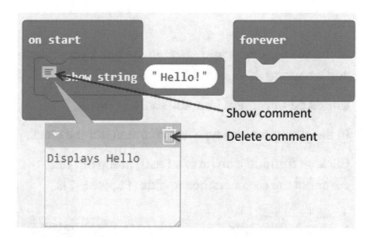

Figure 3-8. Deleting a comment

3-5. Displaying Text

Problem

You want to scroll a text message across the display only once.

Solution

You can use the **on start** block to build this program.

- In the **Toolbox**, click on the **Basic** category.

- Click and drag the **show string** block over and place it inside of the **on start** block. (**Figure 3-9**).

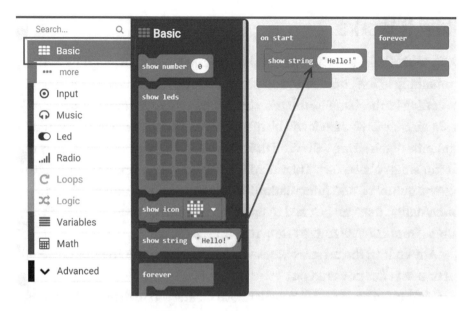

Figure 3-9. *Displaying text*

- The **show string** block contains default text, **Hello!**. If you want to display a different text, simply click on the text box and type in the new text.

- Your final code should look something like this (**Figure 3-10**).

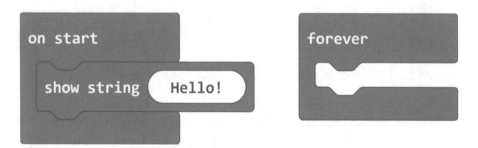

Figure 3-10. *Code listing for display text*

How It Works

With MakeCode, you can use the **show string** block to display any text containing letters, numbers, and punctuation. This is known as a 'string' in coding terms. Usually, the text scrolls from left to right. If the string is a single character, then it will be displayed on the screen; otherwise the contents of the string will scroll from left to right (the micro:bit display only fits for single character). The micro:bit display only supports with English letters, numbers, and punctuation. All the valid letters, numbers, and punctuation that can be used to build a string can be found in the **ASCII table** (*from DEC 32 to 126*) shown in **Appendix A**.

Any code in the **on start** block will run when the micro:bit is powered on or reset after powered on.

MakeCode blocks for micro:bit doesn't allow you to define how fast the string scrolls. If you would like to change the speed, you will need to switch to the JavaScript editor by clicking on the selector at the top of the screen (**Figure 3-11**). Then, in the **basic. showString()** function, type in a comma followed by a value for how fast to shift characters (e.g., 150, 100, 200, −100).

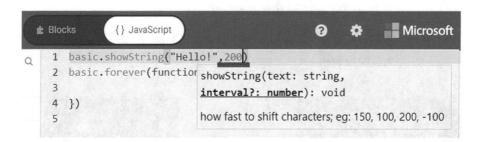

Figure 3-11. *JavaScript equivalent of the code*

You can switch back and forth between **Blocks** and **JavaScript** as you program. If you switched back to the **Blocks**, the **basic.showstring()** block becomes incompatible with **Blocks**. MakeCode uses a gray color to indicate any errors in your code (**Figure 3-12**).

Figure 3-12. *Incompatible Block created by JavaScript*

3-6. Displaying Numbers

Problem

You want to scroll a number across the display only once.

Solution

You can use the **on start** block to build this program.

- In the **Toolbox**, click on the **Basic** category.

- Click and drag the **show number** block over and place it inside of the **on start** block.

- In the **show number** block, simply click on the text box and type in the new number (e.g., 1234). Your code should look something like this (**Figure 3-13**).

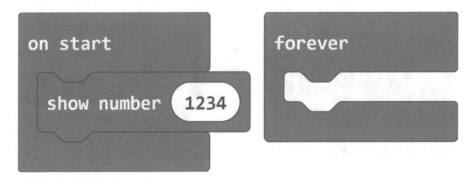

Figure 3-13. *Code listing for display a number*

How It Works

The **on start** block is all your code that will execute at the very beginning of your program and only run once. The show number block accepts digits from 0 to 9. You can build any number with them. It only accepts numbers and digits and doesn't let you type characters and strings. You can't type more than one number in the **show number** block by separating with spaces or punctuation marks. By default, the show number block contains 0. Usually, the numbers scroll from left to right. If the number fits on the display (single digit), it doesn't scroll.

The example in **Figure 3-13** will scroll the number once and then stop if the number is greater than 9. It will not display each number one by one.

3-7. Displaying Text Repeatedly

Problem

You want to display text on micro:bit display, then loop it over and over again.

Solution

You can use the **forever** block to build this program.

- In the **Toolbox**, click on the **Basic** category.

- Click and drag the **show string** block over and place it inside of the **forever** block. Your code should look something like this (**Figure 3-14**).

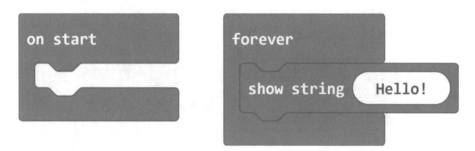

Figure 3-14. *Code listing for display a text*

- If you want to change the ***default text***, click on the textbox of the **show string** block and type in the new text.

How It Works

When you want to repeat anything forever on the micro:bit display, the easiest choice is to use the **forever** block. Simply, it repeats everything placed inside it forever in the background.

3-8. Displaying a Number Repeatedly

Problem

You want to display a number on micro:bit display, then loop it over and over again.

Solution

You can use the **forever** block to build this program.

- In the **Toolbox**, click on the **Basic** category.

- Click and drag the **show number** block over and place it inside of the **forever** block.

- In the **show number** block, click on the text box and type in a number with at least two digits. Your code should look something like this (**Figure 3-15**).

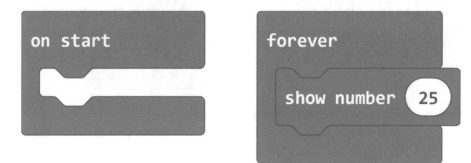

Figure 3-15. *Code listing for display a number repeatedly*

How It Works

When you want to repeat anything forever on the micro:bit display, the easiest choice is to use the **forever** block. Simply, it repeats everything placed inside it forever in the background.

3-9. Turning on LEDs

Problem

You want to turn on some or all LEDs on the micro:bit display.

Solution

You will use the **show leds** block to build the following program.

- In the **Toolbox**, click on the **Basic** category.

- Click and drag the **show leds** block over, and place it inside of the **on start** block (**Figure 3-16**).

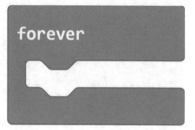

Figure 3-16. *The show leds block*

- In the **show leds** block, click on the squares that you want to select. Your code should look something like this (**Figure 3-17**).

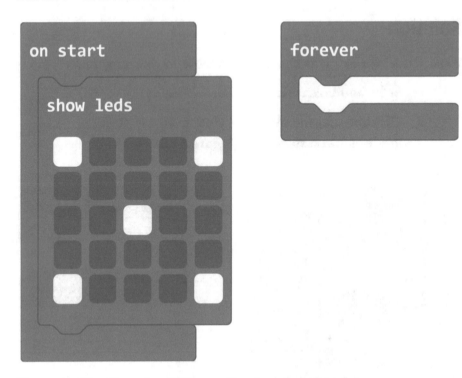

Figure 3-17. *Choosing LEDs on the show leds block*

How It Works

The **show leds** block represents the micro:bit display. Each square in the **show leds** block corresponds to a physical LED on the micro:bit display. You can click on any square to select the corresponding LED on the micro:bit display to turn on. To turn off an LED, simply click on the selected square again to deselect it.

3-10. Displaying Icons

Problem

You want to display one of the built-in icons on the micro:bit display.

Solution

- In the **Toolbox**, click on the **Basic** category.

- Click and drag the **show icon** block over and place it inside of the **on start** block.

- In the **show icon** block, choose an icon (happy) click from the drop-down list to display on the micro:bit screen (**Figure 3-18**).

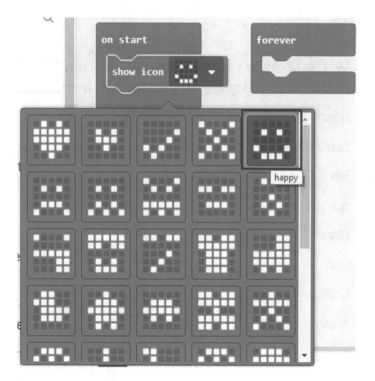

Figure 3-18. *Choosing an icon*

- Your code should look something like this (**Figure 3-19**).

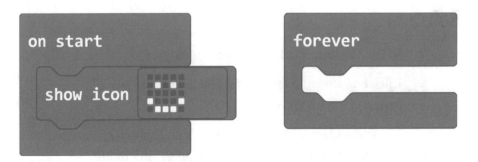

Figure 3-19. *Code listing for display an icon*

How It Works

The show icon block can be used to display an icon at any point in your program. The MakeCode supports 40 icons for your choice. Here is the list:

- Heart
- Small heart
- Yes
- No
- Happy
- Sad
- Confused
- Angry
- Asleep
- Surprised
- Silly
- Fabulous
- Meh

- T-shirt

- Roller skate

- Duck

- House

- Tortoise

- Butterfly

- Stick figure

- Ghost

- Sword

- Giraffe

- Skull

- Umbrella

- Snake

- Rabbit

- Cow

- Quarter note

- Eight note

- Pitchfork

- target

- triangle

- left triangle

- chess board

- diamond

- small diamond

- square

- small square

- scissors

If you want to display more icons sequentially, add more **show icon** blocks to your program. The following program starts with the **heart** icon and stops at the **happy** icon (**Figure 3-20**). If you want to add a delay between icons, use the **pause** block (see **Recipe 3-14, Pausing a Program**).

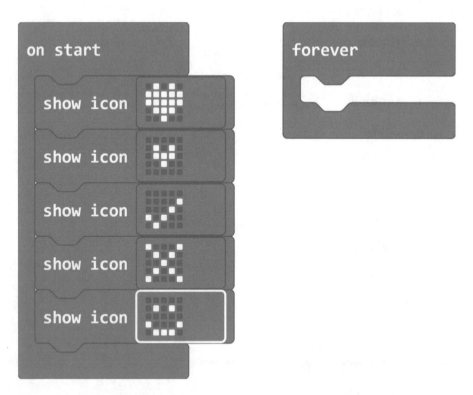

Figure 3-20. *Displaying icons sequentially*

3-11. Displaying Arrows

Problem

You want to draw an arrow pointing to **south east** on the micro:bit display.

Solution

You will use the **show arrow** block to build the following program.

- In the **Toolbox**, click on the **Basic** category, then click the **more** tab.

- Click and drag the **show arrow** block over and place it inside of the **on start** block.

- In the **show arrow** block, choose **south east** from the drop-down list. Your code should look something like this (**Figure 3-21**).

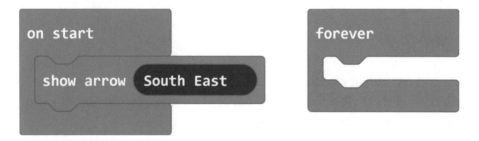

Figure 3-21. *Code listing for display an arrow*

How It Works

The **show arrow** block is *specialized* to display arrows pointing to different directions. The following is a list of directions that can be configured with the show arrow block.

- North

- North East

- East

- South East

- South

- South West

- West

- North West

3-12. Pausing a Program

Problem

You want to pause the execution of a program for several milliseconds that are specified.

Solution

You can use the **pause** block to add a delay between code blocks. As an example, you will display a text containing two words (Hello, World!) and add a 2-second delay between **Hello,** and **World!**

- In the **Toolbox**, click on the **Basic** category.

- Click and drag the **show string** block over and place it inside of the **on start** block.

- Right-click on the **show string** block and from the shortcut menu, click **Duplicate**.

- Change the text of the first **show string** block as **Hello.**

- Change the text of the second **show string** block as **World!**

- Again, click on the **Basic** category. Then click and drag the **pause** block over and place it between the **show string** blocks.

- In the **pause** block, click on the drop-down list and choose **2 seconds (Figure 3-22)**.

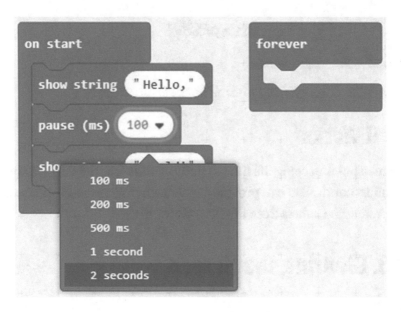

***Figure 3-22.** Adding delay using the pause block*

- Your code should look something like this (**Figure 3-23**).

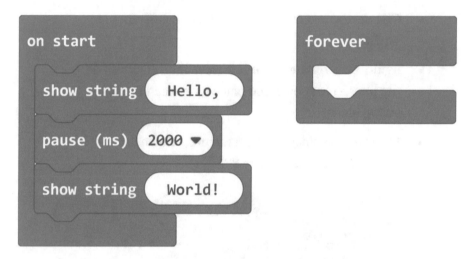

Figure 3-23. *Code listing for adding delay*

How It Works

The **pause** block accepts the time in milliseconds where 1 second equals 1000 milliseconds. You can provide any value in milliseconds or choose some predefined values from the drop-down list.

3-13. Clearing the Screen

Problem

You want to clear the micro:bit display by turning off all the LEDs.

Solution

You can build this program using the **on start** block.

- In the **Toolbox**, click on the Basic category.

- Click and drag the **show string** block over and place it inside of the **on start** block.

- In the **show string** block, click on the text box and type in the letter **X**.

- In the **Toolbox**, under **Basic** category, click on **...more**.

- Click and drag the **clear screen** block over, and place it inside of the **on start** block. Your code should look something like this (**Figure 3-24**).

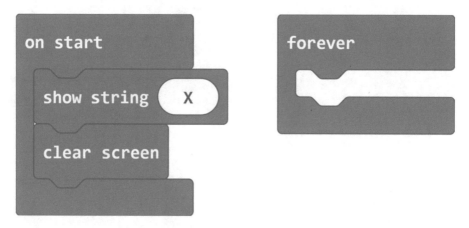

Figure 3-24. *Code listing for clearing the screen*

How It Works

The **clear screen** block allows you to **turn off** all the LEDs in the micro:bit display. You can use it to clear the screen after displaying a text, number, image, icon, or anything.

CHAPTER 4

Working with Text

MakeCode has many blocks to offer when it comes to manipulating text strings. In this chapter you will learn how to find the length of a text, joining together any number of pieces of text, comparing two strings, extracting a part from a string, converting a string to a number, and extracting a character from a string at the specified index.

4-1. Finding the Length of a Text

Problem

You want to find the length of a text.

Solution

- In the **Toolbox**, click on the **Basic** category. Then click and drag the **show number** block over, and place it inside of the **on start** block.

- In the **Toolbox**, click on **Advanced** to expand the category list, and then click on the **Text** category.

- Click and drag the **length of** block over and place it inside of the **show number** block (**Figure 4-1**).

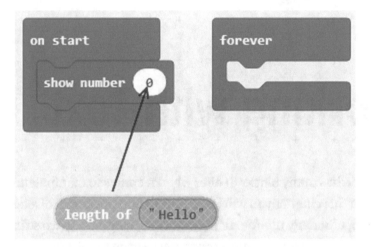

Figure 4-1. *Placing the **length of** block*

- Once finished, your code should look something like this (**Figure 4-2**).

Figure 4-2. *Full code listing*

- The following will be the result.

5

How It Works

The **length of** block returns the number of letters, including spaces in the provided text as an *integer*. Therefore, you must use the **show number** block with the **length of** block to show the output on the micro:bit display.

4-2. Joining Strings

Problem

You want to join two or more strings together to create a piece of text.

Solution

As an example, you will join the following piece of strings to create a text.

You

are

awesome

- In the **Toolbox**, click on the **Basic** category. Then click and drag the **show string** block over, and place it inside of the **on start** block.

- In the **Toolbox**, click on **Advanced** to expand the category list, and then click on the **Text** category.

- Click and drag the **join** block over and place it inside of the **show string** block (**Figure 4-3**).

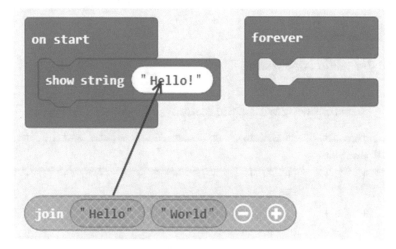

Figure 4-3. *Placing the **join** block*

- In the **join** block, click on the first text box and type the string **You** followed by a space. Then, click on the second text box, and type the string **are** followed by a space.

- Click on the **Add** button (plus icon) to add a new text box (third text box).

- In the third text box, type the string **awesome**.

- Once finished, your code should look something like this (**Figure 4-4**).

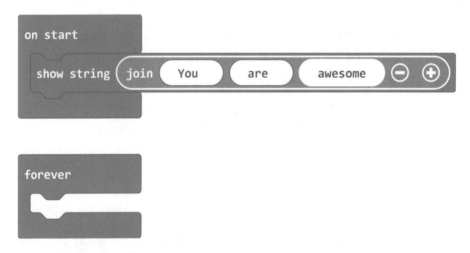

Figure 4-4. *Full code listing*

- The following will be the result.

```
You are awesome
```

How It Works

The **join** block creates a piece of text by joining together any number of strings. It always returns a string. Therefore, you should place it inside a **show string** block to direct the output to the micro:bit display.

The join block comes with two default strings (Hello World). You can add or remove a text box in the **join** block by clicking on the **Add** button (plus icon) or **Remove** button (minus icon), respectively (**Figure 4-5**).

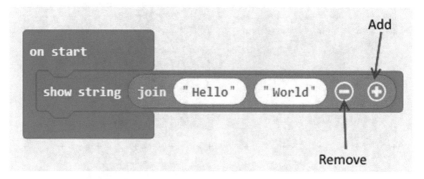

Figure 4-5. *The **join** block*

4-3. Comparing Two Strings

Problem

You want to compare two strings based on which characters are first.

Solution

As an example, you will compare the following two strings.

Apple

Pear

- In the **Toolbox**, click on the **Basic** category. Then click and drag the **show number** block over, and place it inside of the **on start** block.

- In the **Toolbox**, click on **Advanced** to expand the category list, and then click on the **Text** category.

- Click and drag the **compare** block over and place it inside of the **show number** block (**Figure 4-6**).

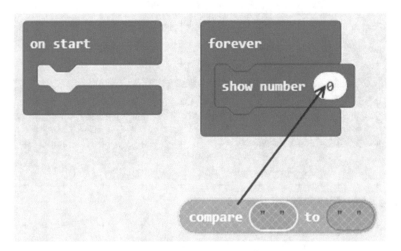

Figure 4-6. *Placing the **compare** block*

- In the **compare** block, click on the first text box and type in the string **Apple**. Then, click on the second text box and type in the string **Pear**.

- Once finished, your code should look something like this (**Figure 4-7**).

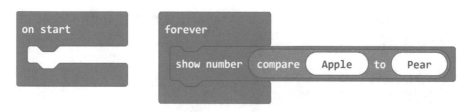

Figure 4-7. *Full code listing*

- The following will be the result.

-1

How It Works

The two strings are compared based on the order of their characters in ASCII encoding. The complete ASCII encoding table with the English alphabet for micro:bit can be found in ***Appendix A***.

Here are some examples that will help you to understand the comparison.

- The string '**A**' is less than '**B**' because 'B' comes after the 'A'.

- The string '**TIGER**' is greater than '**LION**' because '**T**' comes after the '**L**'.

- The string '**Tiger**' is less than '**tiger**' because '**t**' comes after '**T**'.

- The string '**100**' is greater than '**Camel**' because '**C**' comes after '**1**'.

The compare block has two text boxes to type **string1** and **string2** (**Figure 4-8**).

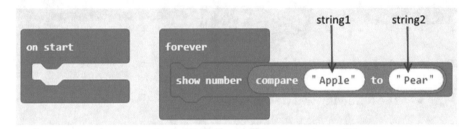

Figure 4-8. *The **compare** block*

The output is based on the following conditions.

- If **string1** *is greater than* **string2**, it returns **1**.

- If both the strings *are equal lexicographically*, it returns **0**.

- If **string1** *is less than* **string2**, it returns **-1**.

You can use the **compare block** with **show number** or **show string** block to direct the output to the micro:bit display.

4-4. Making Substrings

Problem

You want to take some part from a string to make a smaller string.

Solution

As an example, you will take the substring **el** from the string **Hello**.

- In the **Toolbox**, click on the **Basic** category. Then click and drag the **show string** block over, and place it inside of the **on start** block.

- In the **Toolbox**, click on **Advanced** to expand the category list, and then click on the **Text** category.

- Click and drag the **substring of** block over, and place it inside of the **show string** block (**Figure 4-9**).

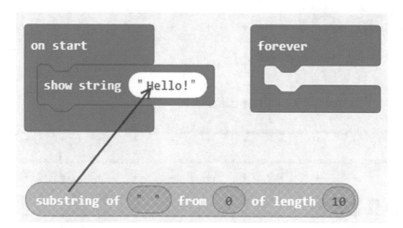

Figure 4-9. *The **substring of** block*

- In the **substring of** block, click on the first text box and type in the string **Hello**. Then, click on the second text box and type in the value **1**. Finally, click on the third text box and type in the value **2**.

- Once finished, your code should look something like this (**Figure 4-10**).

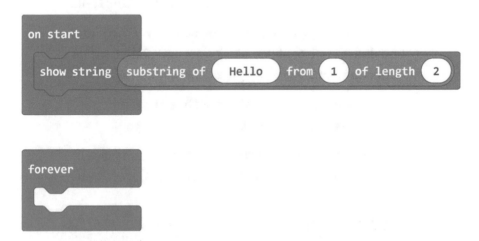

Figure 4-10. *Full code listing*

- The following will be the result.

---

el

How It Works

The **substring of** block can be used to get part of a string. The length of a string is the number of characters it contains, including spaces, punctuation, and control characters. The index of the first character is 0, the second character is 1, and so on. The index of the last character is (length of string) -1.

The first parameter of the **substring of** block accepts the string. The second parameter accepts the index of the first character of the substring. The third parameter accepts the number of characters in the substring, including spaces, punctuation, and control characters.

For example, imagine that you want to get the substring, **'bees'** from the string **'Now I see bees I won'**.

- First, give index for characters in the string (**Figure 4-11**).

Figure 4-11. *Indexing a string*

- Then find the index of the first letter of the substring, which is 10.

- Finally, count the number of characters in the substring, which is 4.

The graphical representation of the substring operation can be illustrated as shown in **Figure 4-12**.

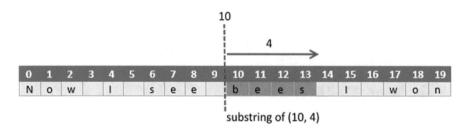

Figure 4-12. *Extracting a part from a string*

Figure 4-13 shows the code for the **Figure 4-12** built with MakeCode.

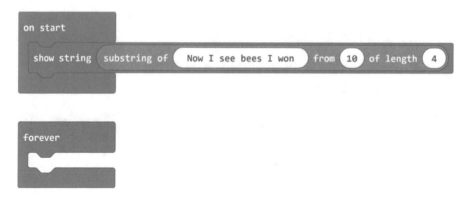

Figure 4-13. *Substring a string*

Here is the list of parameters used for **substring of** block in the **Figure 4-13**.

- **First parameter (substring of)** - complete string, which is **Now I see bees I won**.

- **Second parameter (from)** - index of the first character of the substring, which is **10.**

- **Third parameter (of length)** - number of characters in the substring, which is **4.**

The following will be the result.

---

bees

4-5. Getting a Character at a Position Problem

You want to get a character from a position in the string.

Solution

As an example, you will get the character at the index **1** from the string **Hello**.

- In the **Toolbox**, click on the **Basic** category. Then click and drag the **show string** block over, and place it inside of the **on start** block.

- In the **Toolbox**, click on **Advanced** to expand the category list, and then click on the **Text** category.

- Click and drag the **char from** block over, and place it inside of the **show string** block (**Figure 4-14**).

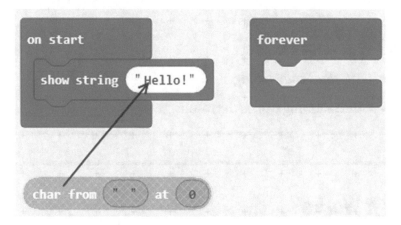

***Figure 4-14.** The **char from** block*

- In the **char from** block, in the first text box, type in the string **Hello**. In the second text box, type in the number **1**.

- Once finished, your code should look something like this (**Figure 4-15**).

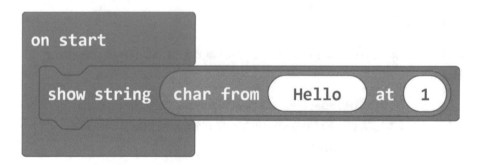

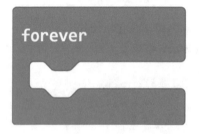

Figure 4-15. *Full code listing*

- The following will be the result.

---

e

How It Works

The **char from** block returns the character at the specified position of any string. The position is known as the index. The index of the first character of the string is 0, the second character is 1, and so on. The index of the last character is (length of string) -1.

The first parameter of the **char from** block accepts the ***input string***. The second parameter accepts the ***index of the character*** that you want to return. A character could be a space, punctuation, or control character.

If you are provided a number that is out of index or negative, the micro:bit display doesn't output anything.

4-6. Converting a String to a Number

Problem

You want to convert a string consisting of number characters to a number value.

Solution

As an example, you will convert the string **-12.5** to the number value, **-12.5**.

- In the **Toolbox**, click on the **Basic** category. Then click and drag the **show number** block over, and place it inside of the **on start** block.

- In the **Toolbox**, click on the **Advanced** to expand the category list and then click on the **Text** category.

- Click and drag the **parse to number** block over and place it inside of the **show number** block (**Figure 4-16**).

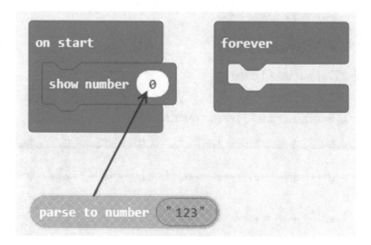

*Figure 4-16. The **parse to number** block*

- In the **parse to number** block, click on the text box and type in the string -**12.5**.

- Once finished, your code should look something like this (**Figure 4-17**).

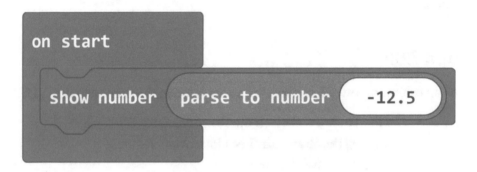

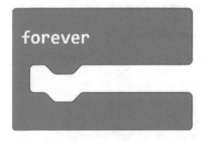

Figure 4-17. *Full code listing*

- The following will be the result.

```
-12.5
```

How It Works

The **parse to number** block allows you to convert a string consisting of number characters into a floating-point number value. The input string can also have a '-' (minus) and '.' (decimal point) symbol. If the first character of the string is the minus symbol, the string will convert into a negative floating-point number value. If your string is something like 123abc, the numeric part will convert to the numeric value, which is 123. If the string is something like abc123, you will get a NaN (Not a Number) error, known as an exception, on the micro:bit display.

Table 4-1 shows the output for strings with different type of character combinations.

Table 4-1. *Output for strings with different type of character combinations*

String	Output
123	123
abc	NaN
123abc	123
abc123	NaN
a123bc	NaN
12 3	12
12-3	12
1.23	1.23
12/3	12

Special Case

If your input string is something like **4e2**, the number characters after the **e** becomes an exponent of **10**. The **2** after the **e** will calculate as **2 powers of ten**, which is **10 * 10** or **100**. The resulting value then is **4 * 100**, which equals **400**. **Figure 4-18** shows the code for calculating the result for **4e2**.

Figure 4-18. *Calculating the result for 4e2*

CHAPTER 5

Displaying Images

This chapter mainly focuses on how to show images on a micro:bit display. MakeCode provides a set of built-in images and image editing blocks to create your own images, limited up to two frames. You can play with images by scrolling and offsetting them in different ways.

5-1. Displaying Built-in Images
Problem

You want to display a built-in image on the micro:bit LED matrix.

Solution

- In the **Toolbox,** click on **Advanced** to expand the category list, and then click on the **Images** category.

- Click and drag the **show image** block over and place it inside of the **on start** block.

- In the **Toolbox,** click on the **Images** category, and then click on the **icon image** block.

- Click and drag the **icon image** block over and place it inside of the **show image** block (**Figure 5-1**).

© Pradeeka Seneviratne 2019
P. Seneviratne, *BBC micro:bit Recipes*, https://doi.org/10.1007/978-1-4842-4913-0_5

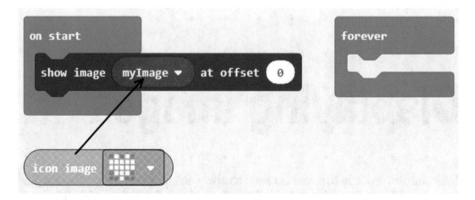

Figure 5-1. *Placing the **icon image** block*

- Click on the **myImage** variable block and from the menu, choose **Delete the "myImage" variable** (**Figure 5-2**).

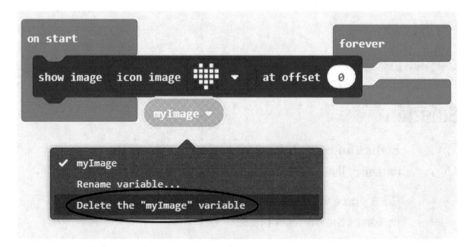

Figure 5-2. *Deleting the **myImage** variable block*

- Click on the **icon image** and from the drop-down menu, choose the **happy** icon. Keep the **offset** as **0** (**Figure 5-3**).

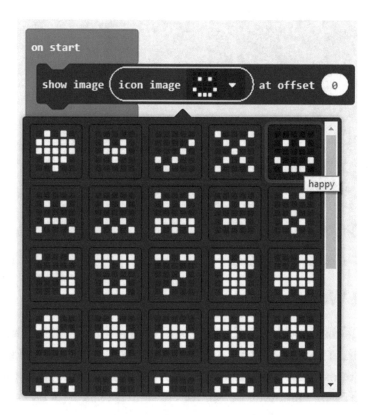

Figure 5-3. *Choosing the **happy** icon*

- Once finished, your code should look something like this (**Figure 5-4**).

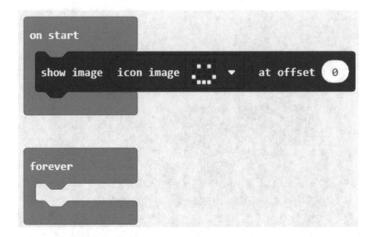

Figure 5-4. *Full code listing*

How It Works

MakeCode comes with 40 built-in images to show on the micro:bit display. The full list of images can be found in **Chapter 2, Recipe 2-1**. MakeCode uses the terms **"icon"** and **"image"** interchangeably. In the **show image** block, the **offset** parameter determines the start position (or end position) of the image to be displayed on the LED matrix.

5-2. Image Offsetting

Problem

You want to shift an image horizontally across the display with offset.

Solution

- In the **Toolbox**, click on **Advanced** to expand the category list, and then click on the **Images** category.

- Click and drag the **show image** block over, and place it inside of the **on start** block.

- In the **Toolbox**, click on the **Images** category, and then click on the **icon image** block.

- Click and drag the **icon image** block over, and place it inside of the **show image** block (**Figure 5-5**).

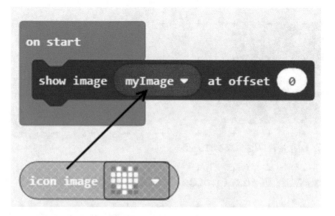

Figure 5-5. *The **show image** block*

- Click on the **myImage** variable block and from the menu, choose **Delete the "myImage" variable**.

- Click on the **icon image** and from the drop-down menu, choose the **happy** icon. Change the **offset** to **2** (**Figure 5-6**).

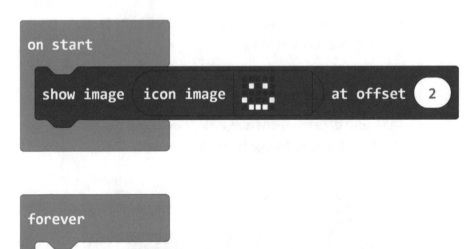

Figure 5-6. *Offsetting an image*

- You will get an output as shown in **Figure 5-7**.

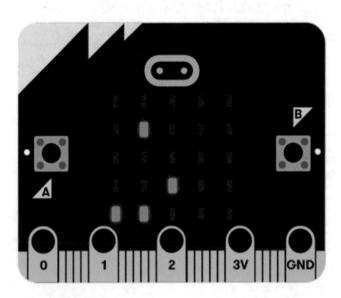

Figure 5-7. *Offsetted output*

How It Works

The micro:bit LED screen consists of 25 LEDs arranged as 5 columns and 5 rows (5 X 5 matrix). The index of the first column is 0 and the last column is 4. The offset allows you to specify the number of LEDs from the left or right of the picture that the micro:bit should start. You can use the following values to make offset for different directions.

- 0 - no offset

- Any positive number - offsets from left

- Any negative number - offsets from right

The LED screen fits in a single frame. A frame is a part of the image. It is a square with five LEDs on a side. An image can span multiple frames. If you use the value 5 or -5 for the offset, you can completely hide the image inside the micro:bit display.

5-3. Scrolling Images
Problem

You want to scroll an image on the micro:bit display with different speeds.

Solution

- In the Toolbox, click on **Advanced** to expand the category list, and then click on the **Images** category.

- Click and drag the **scroll image** block over, and place it inside of the **on start** block.

- In the Toolbox, click on the **Images** category, and then click on the **icon image** block.

- Click and drag the **icon image** block over, and place it inside of the **scroll image** block (**Figure 5-8**).

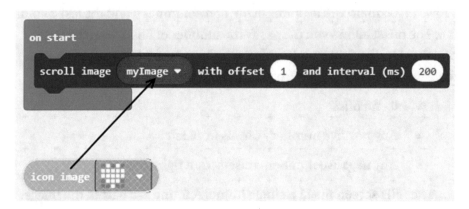

Figure 5-8. *The **scoll image** block*

- Click on the **myImage** variable block and from the menu, choose **Delete the "myImage" variable**.

- Type **2000** for **interval (ms)**.

- Once finished, your code should look something like this (**Figure 5-9**).

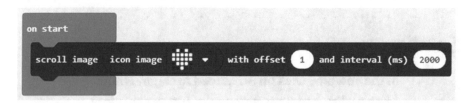

Figure 5-9. *Code listing*

How It Works

The scroll image block allows you to scroll an image on the micro:bit display from right to left or left to right. The offset parameter specifies the number of LEDs from the left or right of the image that the micro:bit should start and continue with the animation. The offset value 0 and 1 does the same effect. The offset 0 and any positive number makes the image scroll from right to left. Any negative number makes the image scroll from left to right. The speed of the scrolling effect can be changed by the interval parameter. It accepts the time in milliseconds.

If you want to repeat the scrolling effect over and over again, place the **scroll image** block inside the **forever** block.

5-4. Creating Your Own Images
Problem

You want to create an image to fit with the micro:bit display.

Solution

- In the Toolbox, click on **Advanced** to expand the category list, and then click on the **Images** category.

- Click and drag the **show image** block over, and place it inside of the **on start** block.

- In the Toolbox, click on the **Images** category, and then click on the **create image** block.

- Click and drag the **create image** block over, and place it inside of the **show image** block (**Figure 5-10**).

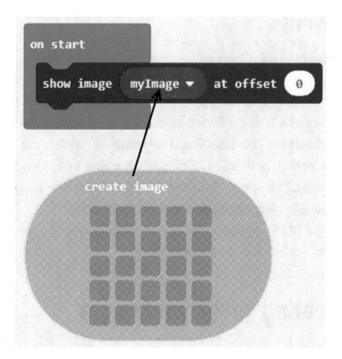

Figure 5-10. *The **create image** block*

- Click on the **myImage** variable block and from the menu, choose **Delete the "myImage" variable** (**Figure 5-11**).

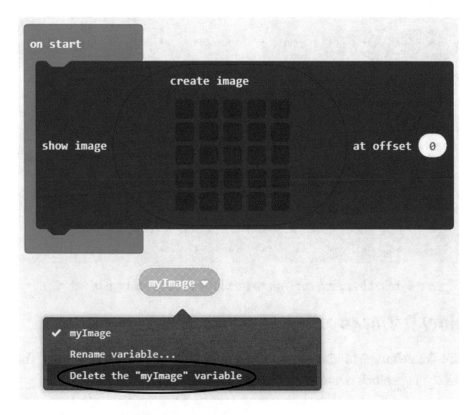

Figure 5-11. *Deleting the **myImage** variable block*

- In the **create image** block, click on the LEDs to
  create the image that you want (e.g., robot) as shown in
  Figure 5-12.

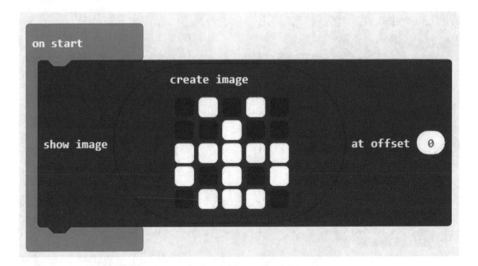

Figure 5-12. *Creating an image with the **create image** block*

How It Works

The create image block represents the micro:bit's physical LED screen. The 5 X 5 image block is known as a single frame image.

5-5. Creating a Double-Sized Image

Problem

You want to create a large image with two frames.

Solution

- In the **Toolbox**, click on **Advanced** to expand the category list, and then click on the **Images** category.

- Click and drag the **show image** block over, and place it inside of the **on start** block.

- In the **Toolbox**, click on the **Images** category, and then click on the **create big image** block.

- Click and drag the **create big image** block over, and place it inside of the **show image** block (**Figure 5-13**).

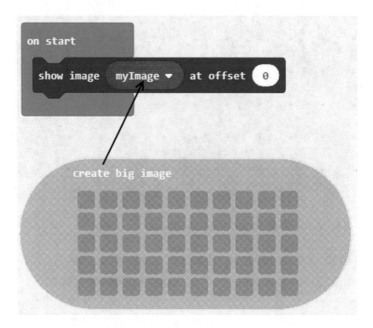

Figure 5-13.   *The create big image block*

- Click on the **myImage** variable block and from the drop-down list, choose **Delete the "myImage" variable** (**Figure 5-14**).

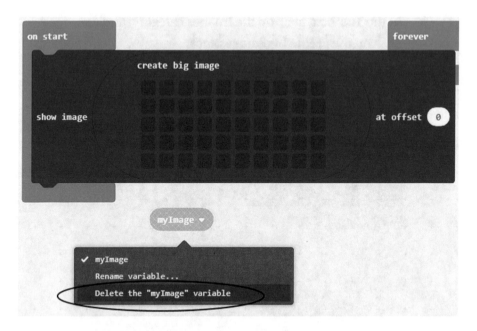

Figure 5-14. *Deleting **myImage** variable*

- In the create big image block, draw two images
  (giraffes) by clicking on the squares (**Figure 5-15**).

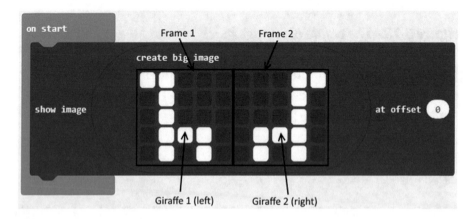

Figure 5-15. *Image frames*

- When you run the code on micro:bit, you can only see the **Giraffe 1 (left)** in **Frame 1** on the micro:bit display (**Figure 5-16**).

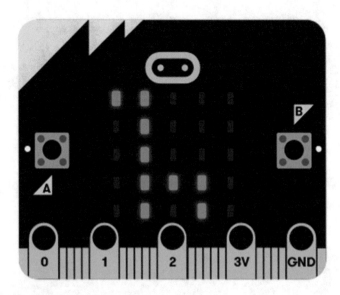

Figure 5-16. *Output on the LED screen*

How It Works

MakeCode allows you to create images with two frames. Each frame consists of 5 rows and five columns of LEDs. When you run the code on the micro:bit, the micro:bit display will show the first frame of the image. If you want to see the second frame, you should use **offset** or **scroll** methods.

Figure 5-17 shows the code for displaying Frame 2 using the offset method. You should type the index of the first column of the second frame, which is **5** in the **offset** box.

Figure 5-17. *Using the **show image** block*

Figure 5-18 shows how to use the scroll image block to display Frame 2 on the micro:bit LED screen.

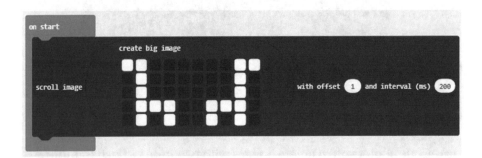

Figure 5-18. *Using the **scroll image** block*

5-6. Displaying Arrows

Problem

You want to display an arrow pointing to the **south west** direction.

Solution

- In the **Toolbox**, click **Advanced** followed by **Images**. Then click and drag the **show image** block over and place it inside of the **on start** block.

- In the **Toolbox**, click **Images** again. Then click and drag the **arrow image** block over, and place it inside of the **show image** block (**Figure 5-19**).

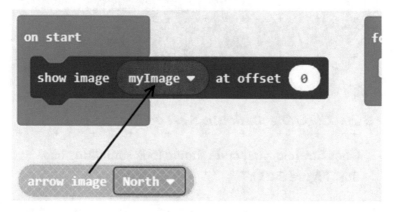

Figure 5-19. *Placing the **arrow image** block*

- Click on the **myImage** variable and from the drop-down list, choose **Delete the "myImage" variable**.

- In the **arrow image** block, click on the drop-down list and choose the **South West** option (**Figure 5-20**).

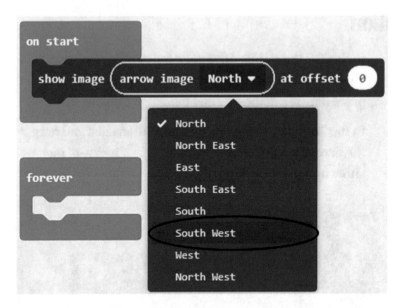

Figure 5-20. *Choosing the **South West** option*

- Once finished, your code should look something like this (**Figure 5-21**).

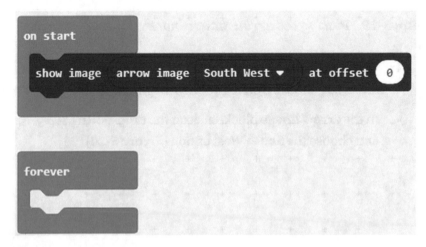

Figure 5-21. *Full code listing*

- **Figure 5-22** shows the output.

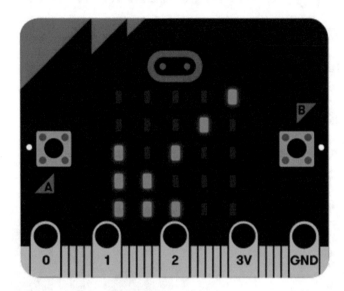

Figure 5-22. Output on the LED screen

How It Works

The **arrow image** block allows you to display an arrow pointing to different directions. It is the only *image group* that you can find in the MakeCode for micro:bit. It has the following set of arrows.

- North
- North East
- East
- South East
- South
- South West
- West
- North West

5-7. Using Variable to Hold an Image

Problem

You want to use a variable to hold an image.

Solution

- In the **Toolbox**, click on the **Variables** category, and then click on **Make a Variable... (Figure 5-23).**

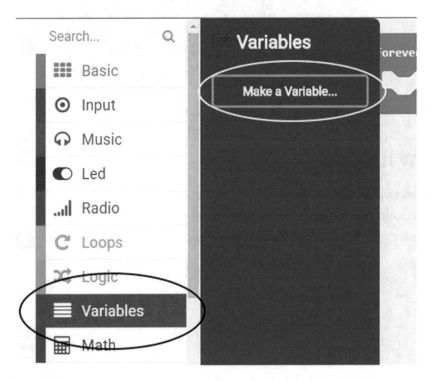

Figure 5-23. *Creating a variable*

- In the **New variable name** modal box (window), type in the variable name (e.g., **heart**). Then click on the **Ok** button (**Figure 5-24**).

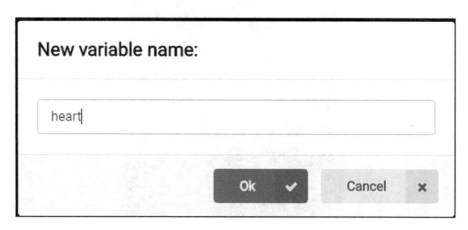

Figure 5-24. *Providing a name for the variable*

- Now your **Variables Toolbox** should look something like this (**Figure 5-25**). It contains the variable and two blocks to set and change the variable.

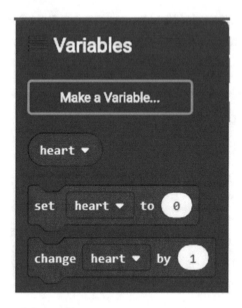

Figure 5-25. *Variable toolbox*

- Now click and drag the **set heart to** block over and place it inside of the **on start** block.

- In the **Toolbox**, click **Advanced** followed by **Images**. Then click and drag the **icon image** block over, and place it inside of the **set heart to** block (**Figure 5-26**).

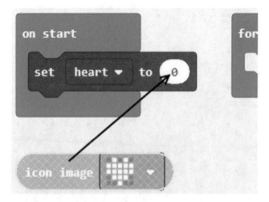

Figure 5-26. *Assigning an icon image to a variable*

- In the **Toolbox**, click **Images**. Then click and drag the **show image** block over and place it inside of the **forever** block.

- In the **show image** block, click on the **myImage** and from the drop-down list, choose the variable, **heart** (**Figure 5-27**).

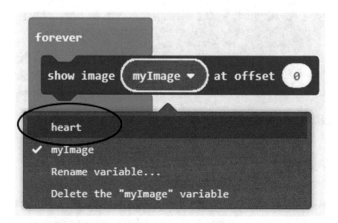

Figure 5-27. *Choosing the variable,* ***heart***

- Now your code should look something like this (**Figure 5-28**).

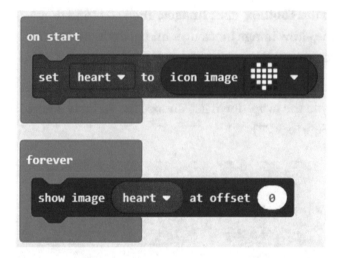

Figure 5-28. *Full code listing*

How It Works

Variables can hold built-in images and custom images. Once assigned an image to a variable, you can use the variable name to display the image at any point in your code.

CHAPTER 6

Inputs and Outputs

In this chapter, you learn how to handle inputs and outputs with micro:bit through the edge connector. The 21 I/O pins can be used to work with analog, digital, I2C, SPI, and UART. Some I/O pins are also specialized to build touch-sensitive applications. The micro:bit only exposes three I/O pins through the edge connector for basic users. If you want to access the full set of I/O pins, you can use an edge connector breakout.

6-1. Using Edge Connector
Problem

You want to connect the pins 0, 1, 2, 3V, and GND to an external component.

Solution

Connect the external components (or circuit) to the micro:bit with Alligator/Crocodile clips (sometimes called Alligator/Crocodile leads) as shown in **Figure 6-1**.

© Pradeeka Seneviratne 2019
P. Seneviratne, *BBC micro:bit Recipes*, https://doi.org/10.1007/978-1-4842-4913-0_6

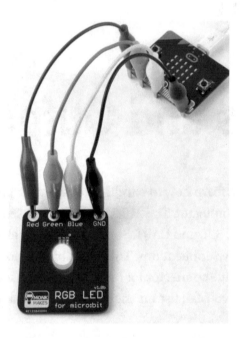

Figure 6-1. *Using Alligator/Crocodile clips with the edge connector (Image courtesy of Monk Makes: https://www.monkmakes.com)*

How It Works

The micro:bit exposes its I/O pins through the edge connector, as shown in **Figure 6-2**. The edge connector consists of large and small connection pads. The large connection pads expose GPIO pins 0, 1, and 2 only. Apart from that, you can find 3V and GND pads that can be used to power up your sensors, actuators, and external circuits.

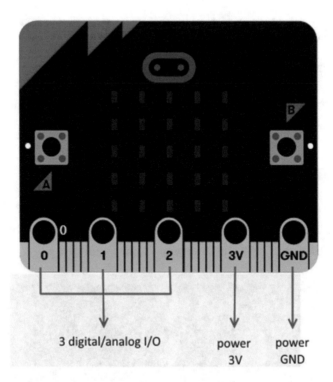

Figure 6-2. *I/O pins*

These alligator/crocodile clips are cheap, easy to use, and don't require any extra skills to connect them with the edge connector. You can purchase bundles of these cables from various electronic resellers:

- **MonkMakes** (https://www.monkmakes.com/mb-alligator-short/)

- **Kitronik** (https://www.kitronik.co.uk/2407-crocodile-leads-pack-of-10.html)

- **SparkFun** (https://www.sparkfun.com/products/12978)

These clips are not very stable and can lose the connection or touch with other pins in the edge connector, resulting in a short circuit or overheating of the processor.

6-2. Using Edge Connector Breakout

Problem

You want to connect an external circuit to the small pads in the edge connector.

Solution

Figure 6-3 shows how to insert the micro:bit into the Kitronik edge connector breakout. Make sure to insert it firmly into the slot of the edge connector breakout, and the micro:bit should be **face up**.

Figure 6-3. *Kitronik edge connector breakout (Image courtesy of Kitronik: https://www.kitronik.co.uk/)*

How It Works

Alligator/Crocodile leads can't be used to connect with small pads in the edge connector. As a solution, you can use an edge connector breakout to access all the 21 I/O pins. Usually edge connector breakouts break the micro:bit edge connector into a row of pin headers. Here is the list of manufacturers and vendors:

- **Kitronik** (https://www.kitronik.co.uk/5601b-edge-connector-breakout-board-for-bbc-microbit-pre-built.html)

- **SparkFun** (https://www.sparkfun.com/products/13989)

- **Waveshare** (https://www.aliexpress.com/item/Waveshare-Edge-connector-expansion-board-for-micro-bit-breakout-the-I-O-pins-to-2-54mm/32864979980.html)

6-3. Using Built-In Buttons

Problem

You want to display different images by pressing the buttons A and B for all the possible combinations.

Solution

- In the **Toolbox**, click on the **Variables** category and then click on the **Make a variable...** button.

- In the **New variable name** modal box (window), type "**a**" without the double quotation marks. Then click on the **Ok** button to create the variable.

- Repeat the above step to create two more variables, "**b**"
  and "**ab**" (without double quotes) (**Figure 6-4**).

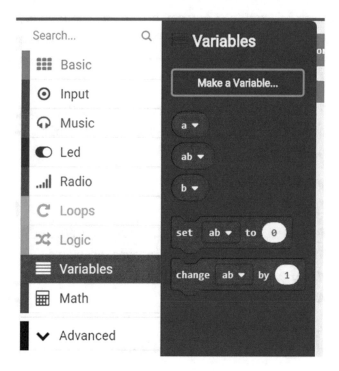

Figure 6-4. *Variables toolbox*

- In the **Toolbox**, click on the **Variables** category. Then
  click and drag the **set *variable* to** block over and place
  it inside to the **on start** block. After that, choose the
  variable "**a**" from the drop-down list.

- In the **Toolbox**, click the **Images** category. Then click
  and drag the **icon image** block over and place it inside
  the **set *variable* to** block. After that, choose the **happy**
  icon from the drop-down list.

- Repeat the above two steps to add and configure two more **set *variable* to** blocks for the variables "**b**" and "**ab**." Also, choose "**sad**" and "**confused**" icons, respectively, for the **set *variable* to** blocks (**Figure 6-5**).

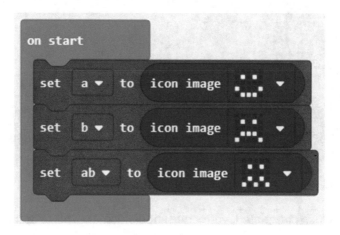

Figure 6-5. *Assigning icons to variables*

- In the **Toolbox**, click the **Input** category and click on the **on button *x* pressed** block. Then choose the button "**A**" from the drop-down list if it has not already selected by default.

- In the **Toolbox**, click on the **Images** category. Then click and drag the **show image** block over and place it inside the **on button A pressed** block. After that, choose the variable "**a**" from the drop-down list if it has not already selected by default.

- Repeat the above two steps for the **on button B pressed** and **on button AB pressed** event handlers (**Figure 6-6**).

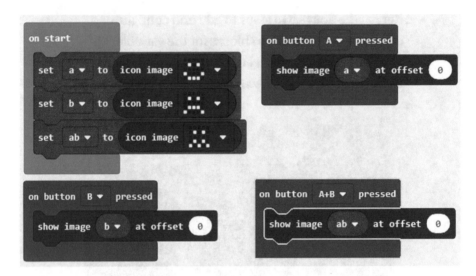

Figure 6-6.   Using button press event handlers

- Once completed, your code shook look like this (**Figure 6-7**).

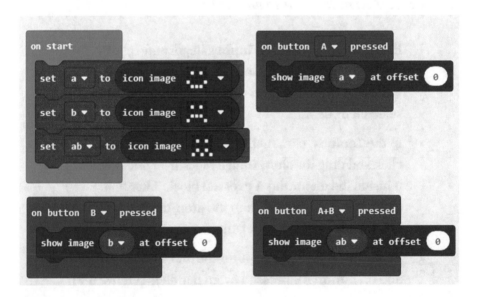

Figure 6-7.   Full code listing

How It Works

There are two momentary push buttons on the front side of the micro:bit labeled as **A** and **B** (**Figure 6-8**).

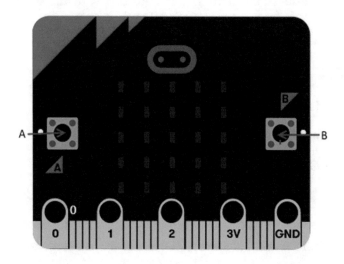

Figure 6-8. *Built-in two momentary push buttons A and B. The third button can be simulated by pressing button A and B together.*

Button A is internally connected to digital pin 5, and button B is internally connected to digital pin 11. MakeCode provides three ***event handlers*** to detect when these buttons are pressed. They are the following:

- on button A pressed
- on button B pressed
- on button A+B pressed (press both buttons together)

These event handlers allow you to trigger a piece of code during the program execution. The variable **a** holds the icon image for the **button A.** The variable **b** holds the icon image for the **button B**. The variable **ab** holds the icon image for both **buttons A+B**.

6-4. Using External Buttons

Problem

You want to connect a momentary push button to the micro:bit to read inputs.

Solution

You will need the following components to build the circuit:

- Momentary push button

- 1k Ohm resistor

- 4 Alligator Leads (https://www.monkmakes.com/product/)

Wire up the momentary push button with the pull-up resistor and connect the button with micro:bit pin 0 as shown in **Figure 6-9**.

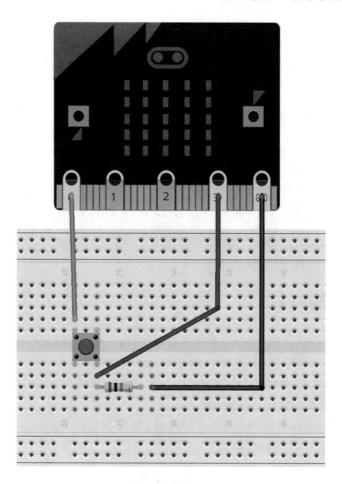

Figure 6-9. *Connecting an external push button with Pin0*

- In the MakeCode **Toolbox**, click **Input**. Then click on the **on pin x pressed** block. Choose **P0** from the drop-down list if it has not already been selected.

- In the **Toolbox**, click **Basic** and then click and drag the show icon block over, and place it inside the **on pin P0 pressed** block.

- Once completed, your code should look something like this (**Figure 6-10**).

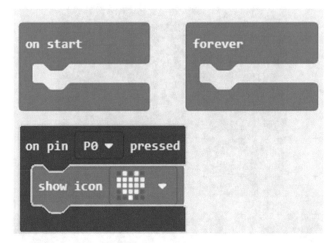

Figure 6-10. *Full code listing*

How It Works

With MakeCode, you can use micro:bit pins 0, 1, and 2 to connect with external buttons to read inputs using on **pin x pressed** block. These pins are labeled as P0, P1, and P2, respectively. They can be found in the edge connector of the micro:bit board.

Typically, a momentary push button has four pins that can be labeled as A, B, C, and D (**Figure 6-11**).

Figure 6-11. *Pinout of the momentary push button*

The following pins are internally connected (**Figure 6-12**).

- A and D

- B and C

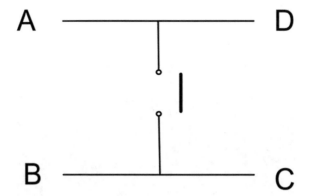

Figure 6-12. *Internal connection between pins*

These switches are normally in the OPEN state, and they must be pushed to complete or CLOSE the circuit. The circuit can be completed through AB, CD, AC, or BD.

Make sure to connect external buttons with the micro:bit using pull-up circuits. This will allow you to cut off electrical noise interference and provide accurate on-off readings.

6-5. Controlling Brightness of an LED

Problem

You want to control the brightness of an LED with a potentiometer.

Solution

You will need the following things to build the circuit:

- 10K Ohm potentiometer

- 3 mm LED

- 4 Alligator leads

Figure 6-13 presents the wiring diagram for the circuit.

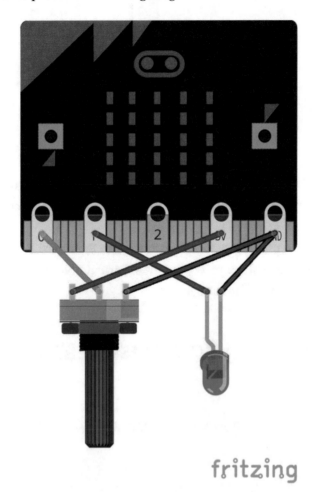

Figure 6-13. *Wiring diagram for analog read/write circuit*

Follow these steps to wire the circuit:

- Connect the positive lead of the LED to the micro:bit pin 1.

- Connect the negative lead of the LED to the micro:bit GND pin.

- Connect the middle pin of the potentiometer to the micro:bit pin 0.

- Connect one of the outer pins of the potentiometer to the micro:bit 3V.

- Connect the other outer pin of the potentiometer to the micro:bit GND pin.

Also, follow these steps to build the code with MakeCode:

- In the **Toolbox**, click on the **Pins** category. Next, click and drag the **analog write pin** block over and place it inside the **forever** block. Then choose, **P1** from the drop-down menu.

- In the **Toolbox**, click on the **Pins** category again. Then click and drag the **analog read pin** block over and place it inside the *placeholder* of the **analog write pin** block. Choose **P0** from the drop-down menu if it has not already been selected.

- Once completed, your code should look like this (**Figure 6-14**).

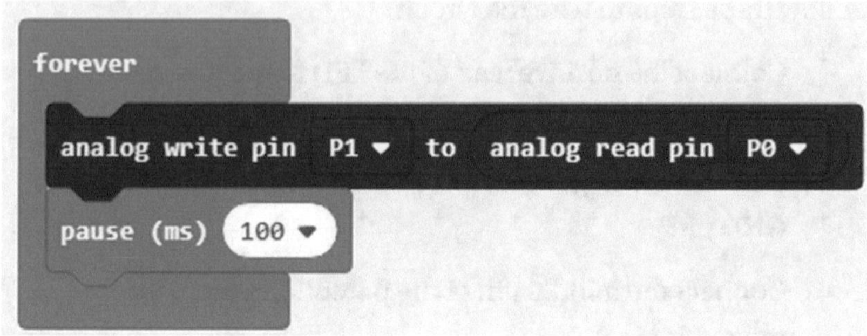

Figure 6-14. *Full code listing*

How It Works

When you turn the shaft of the potentiometer, the voltage at the center pin will change. The same effect will happen at the micro:bit pin 0. You can read the voltage at the center pin with the **analog read pin** block and write the same value at pin 1 to change the brightness of the LED using an **analog write pin** block.

The analog read pin block returns an integer between 1–1023. The same value can be passed to the analog write pin to control the voltage at pin 1, which controls the brightness of the attached LED.

The following steps show you how to calculate the voltage on pin 1 for an analog value 500 on pin 0.

- First, calculate the voltage for the analog read value 1 by dividing the maximum voltage, 3V, by 1023.

  3.0 / 1023 = 0.002932551V

- Then multiply this result by 500:

  0.002932551 x 500 = 1.46

- So, a value of 500 will send 1.46 volts into pin 1.

6-6. Using Digital Input and Output

Problem

You want to turn an LED on and off based on the button status.

Solution

You will need the following things to build the circuit:

- Momentary push button

- 3 mm LED

- 4 Alligator leads

Figure 6-15 presents the wiring diagram for the circuit.

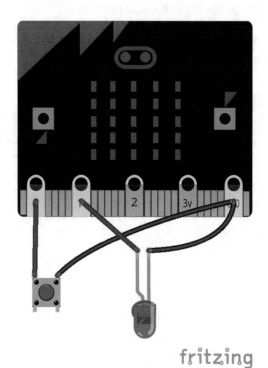

Figure 6-15. *Wiring diagram for digital read/write circuit*

Follow these steps to wire the circuit.

- In the **Toolbox**, click on the **Pins** category. Now, click and drag the **digital write pin** block over and place it inside the **forever** block. Then choose **P1** from the drop-down menu.

- In the **Toolbox**, click on the **Pins** category. Now, click and drag the **digital read pin** block over and place it inside the *placeholder* of the **digital write pin** block. Then choose **P0** from the drop-down menu if it has not already been selected.

- In the **Toolbox**, click on the **Basic** category. Then click and drag the **pause (ms)** block over and place it underneath the **digital write pin** block.

- Once completed, your code should look like this (**Figure 6-16**).

Figure 6-16. *Full code listing*

How It Works

Digital signals or data can be expressed as a series of 0 and 1 digits. **Figure 6-17** shows a digital signal with two statuses over time. The voltage level of HIGH takes 3.3V and LOW takes 0V.

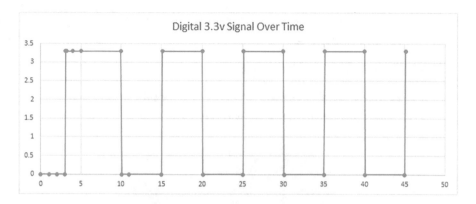

Figure 6-17. *Digital 3.3V signal over time*

In the above example, when you press and hold the push button, the **digital read pin** returns 1. When you release it, the **digital read pin** returns 0. The return value of the **digital read pin** is used as the input for the **digital write pin** to turn on and off the LED; when the **digital write pin** receives 1, the LED will turn on. When the **digital write pin** receives 0, the LED will turn off.

6-7. Writing a Number to a Device at a I2C Address

Problem

You want to write the value 255 to a device at a I2C address 0x1d as an 8-bit number.

Solution

- In the **Toolbox**, click on the **Pins** category. Then click and drag the **i2c write number** block over and place it inside the **on start** block.

- Type the value **29** for the **at address** parameter.

- Type the value **255** for the **with value** parameter.

- Choose **Int8LE** from the drop-down menu for the **format** parameter.

- Choose **false** for the **repeated** parameter.

- **Figure 6-18** shows the i2c write number block configured with all the required parameters.

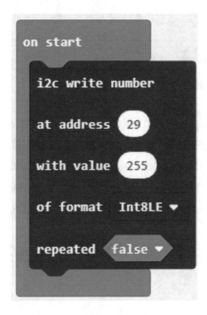

*Figure 6-18. The **i2c write number** block*

How It Works

The micro:bit supports with the I2C (Inter-Integrated Circuit) communication protocol that allows you to connect devices through the I2C bus. You can use SDA and SCL pins of the micro:bit to connect devices and communicate through the I2C bus. Therefore, I2C requires two wires to communicate.

Depending on the configuration, the I2C bus can support up to 1024 slave devices; however as 7 bit addressing is used with micro:bit

MicroPython, the amount of slave devices is 128. **Figure 6-19** shows the communication paths between master and slave devices of a I2C bus.

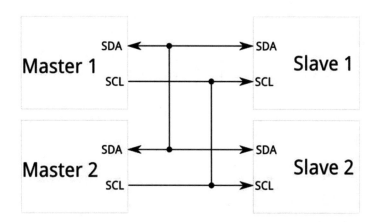

Figure 6-19. *Master and slave devices connected through the I2C bus*

In the above example, the on-board accelerometer of the micro:bit, which is internally connected with the I2C bus at the address 0x1d, is used to write numbers using MakeCode. The decimal equivalent of the 0x1d (in hex) is 29.

Here is the list of parameters that can be used with the i2c write number block:

- **address**: the 7-bit I2C address of the device to send to send value to.

- **value**: the number to send to the address.

- **format**: the Number Format for value. You can learn more about the number formats by visiting `https://makecode.microbit.org/types/buffer/number-format`.

- **repeated**: if true, don't send a stop condition after the write. Otherwise, a stop condition is sent when false (the default).

6-8. Reading a Number from a Device at a I2C Address

Problem

You want to read a number from the device at a 7-bit I2C address 0x1d as an 8-bit number.

Solution

- In the **Toolbox**, click on the **Basic** category. Then click and drag the **show number** block over and place it inside the **on start** block.

- In the **Toolbox**, click on the **Pins** category. Then click and drag the **i2c read number** block over and place it inside the *placeholder* of the **show number** block.

- Type the value **29** for the device address.

- Choose **Int8LE** for the number format.

- Choose **false** for repeated.

- **Figure 6-20** shows the i2c write number block configured with all the required parameters.

*Figure 6-20.   The **i2c read number** block*

How It Works

In above example, the **i2c read number** block reads one byte from the device connected to the I2C bus at the address 0x1d.

6-9. Writing Data to an SPI Slave Device

Problem

You want to write a data value to the SPI slave device.

Solution

- In the Toolbox, click on the Pins category. Next, click and drag the spi set pins block over and place it inside the on start block. Then choose P15 for MOSI, P14 for MISO, and P13 for SCK.

- In the Toolbox, click on the Pins category. Next, click and drag the spi format bits block over and place it underneath the spi set pins block. Then type 8 for bits and 3 for mode.

- In the Toolbox, click on the Pins category. Next, click and drag the spi frequency block over and place it underneath the spi format bits block. Then type 1000000 for frequency.

- In the Toolbox, click on the Basic category. Then click and drag the show number block over and place it underneath the spi frequency block.

- In the Toolbox, click on the Pins category. Next, click and drag the spi write block over and place it inside the placeholder of the show number block. Then type 64 in the number box.

- **Figure 6-21** shows the completed code.

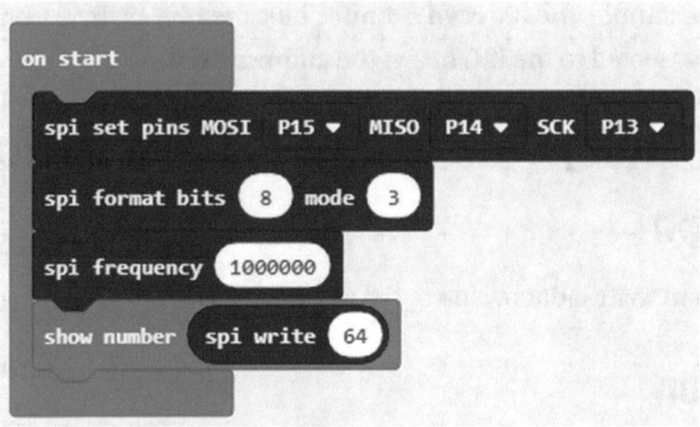

Figure 6-21. Full code listing

How It Works

The **SPI** (Serial Peripheral Interface) allows you to connect devices with the micro:bit through the SPI bus. The SPI uses master-slave architecture with a single master device. The SPI requires three wires to communicate between master and slave. They are:

- SCLK: Serial Clock (output from master).

- MOSI: Master Output, Slave Input (output from master).

- MISO: Master Input, Slave Output (output from slave).

There is a separate line used for CS (Chip Select), and it can be any digital pin in the edge connector of the micro:bit.

The **spi write** block accepts a number that is the data value to send to the SPI slave device. Also, the **spi write** block returns a number value, which is the response from the SPI slave device. Before starting, write any value to an SPI slave device; you must configure and set some important parameters using the following blocks.

- **spi set pins** – Set the Serial Peripheral Interface (SPI) signaling pins. An SPI connection uses hreee signaling lines called MOSI, MISO, and SCK. If you don't set the pins for the SPI connection, the default pin assignments are used:

  - P15 = MOSI, micro:bit SPI data output pin

  - P14 = MISO, micro:bit SPI data input pin

  - P13 = SCK, micro:bit SPI serial clock output pin

- **spi frequency** – Sets the Serial Peripheral Interface (SPI) clock frequency. The default clock frequency is 1 Mhz (10000000 Hz). You can set the frequency for the SPI connection to some other value if you need a different data rate.

- **spi format** – Sets the Serial Peripheral Interface (SPI) format. The bits parameter is used to set the number of bits to represent each value. The mode parameter presents a mode value for the SPI clock (SCK) signaling. Following are the different types of modes you can use:

  - **0**: the data line is active when SCK goes to high, and the data values are read when SCK goes to high.

  - **1**: the data line is active when SCK goes to high, and the data values are read when SCK goes to low.

  - **2**: the data line is active when SCK goes to low, and the data values are read when SCK goes to high.

  - **3**: the data line is active when SCK goes to low, and the data values are read when SCK goes to low.

CHAPTER 7

Loops and Logic

This chapter presents some recipes about how to use loops and logic with MakeCode. MakeCode provides four type of loops to continually repeat blocks until a certain condition is reached:

- repeat
- while
- for
- for element

It also provides three types of block categories for decision making:

- conditional
- comparison
- Boolean

7-1. Repeating Some Code Blocks Several Times

Problem

You want to display numbers from 1 to 10 using a loop.

© Pradeeka Seneviratne 2019
P. Seneviratne, *BBC micro:bit Recipes*, https://doi.org/10.1007/978-1-4842-4913-0_7

Solution

- In the **Toolbox**, click the **Variables** category. Then click on the **Make a Variable...** button. In the **New variable name** modal box, type **x**. Then click on the **Ok** button.

- Again, click on the **Variables** category, and then click and drag the **set *variable* to** block over and place it inside the **on start** block. Then choose the variable name **x** from the drop-down list if it has not already been selected. Also type **1** for the *initial value*.

- In the **Toolbox**, click the **Loops** category. Then click and drag the **repeat *n* times** block over again, and place it inside the **on start** block just below the **set *variable* to** block. Type **10** for the number of times that you want to repeat the action.

- In the **Toolbox**, click the **Basic** category. Then click and drag the **show number** block over, and place it inside the **repeat *10* times** block. Choose the variable **x** from the drop-down list if it has not already been selected.

- In the **Toolbox**, click the **Variables** category. Then click and drag the **change *variable* by** block over, and place it inside the **repeat *10* times** block just below the **show number** block. Choose the variable **x** from the drop-down list if it has not already been selected.

- Once completed, your code should look something like this (**Figure 7-1**).

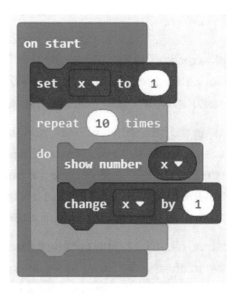

Figure 7-1. *Full code listing*

How It Works

The **repeat n times** block allows you to execute a group of blocks several times. The ***number of times*** can be defined in the text box of the **repeat *n* times** block.

7-2. Run a Same Sequence of Actions While a Condition Is Met

Problem

You want to print numbers from 1 to 10 using a while loop.

Solution

- In the **Toolbox**, click the **Variables** category. Then click on the **Make a Variable...** button. In the **New variable name** modal box, type **x**. Then click on the **Ok** button.

- Again, click on the **Variables** category, and then click and drag the **set *variable* to** block over and place it inside the **on start** block. Then choose the variable name **x** from the drop-down list if it has not already been selected. Also type **1** for the ***initial value***.

- In the **Toolbox**, click the **Loops** category. Then click and drag the **while-do** block over again, and place it inside the **on start** block just below the **set *variable* to** block.

- In the while block, choose the variable x from the first drop-down list. Then choose less than or equal ($\leq$) from the second drop-down list for the condition. After that, type **10** in the text box for the value you want to compare with the result using the condition.

- In the **Toolbox**, click the **Basic** category. Then click and drag the **show number** block over, and place it inside the **while-do** block. Choose the variable **x** from the drop-down list if it has not already been selected.

- In the **Toolbox**, click the **Variables** category. Then click and drag the **change *variable* by** block over, and place it inside the **while-do** block just below the **show number** block. Choose the variable **x** from the drop-down list if it has not already been selected.

- Once completed, your code should look something like this (**Figure 7-2**).

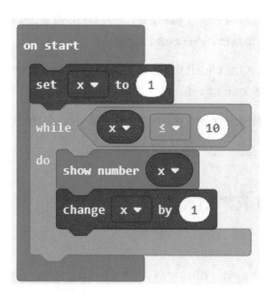

Figure 7-2. *Full code listing*

How It Works

The **while-do** loop allows you to ***repeat*** a block until a specific condition is met. In the above example, the while loop prints numbers from 1 and increments by 1 in each step until the result is less than or equal to 10 where 10 is considered as the condition. In each step, the show number block prints the result, and the change **x** by 1 block increments the result by 1.

The while-do block supports the following conditions.

- =   Return true if both inputs are equal each other.

- ≠   Return true if both inputs are not equal to each other.

- <   Return true if the first input is smaller than the second input.

- ≤   Return true if the first input is smaller than or equal to the second input.

- >   Return true if the first input is greater than the second input.

- ≥   Return true if the first input is greater than or equal to the second input.

7-3. Using *for* Loop

Problem

You want to display even numbers from 0 to 10 on the micro:bit screen.

Solution

- In the **Toolbox**, click the **Variables** category. Then click on the **Make a Variable...** button. In the **New variable name** modal box, type **x**. Then click on the **Ok** button.

- In the **Toolbox**, click on the **Variables** category again. Then click and drag the **set *variable* to** block over, and place it inside the **on start** block. Choose the variable **x** from the drop-down list.

- In the **Toolbox,** click the **Loops** category. Then click and drag the **for** block over, and place it inside the **on start** block just below the **set *variable* to** block. In the textbox, type **5** for the end number (end step).

- In the **Toolbox**, click the **Basic** category. Then click and drag the **show number** block over, and place it inside the **for** block. Choose the variable **x** from the dropdown list.

- In the **Toolbox**, click the **Variables** category. Then click and drag the **change** *variable* **by** block over, and place it inside the **for** block just below the **show number** block. Choose the variable **x** from the drop-down list, and type 2 for the increment value.

- Once completed, your code should look something like this (**Figure 7-3**).

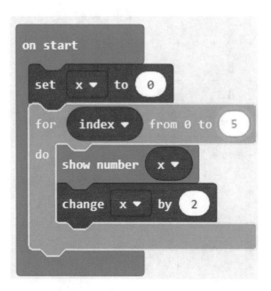

Figure 7-3. *Full code listing*

How It Works

The *for* loop allows you to run same code over and over again, the number of times you specify. In the above solution under Recipe 7-3, the for loop repeats the code 6 times (0 to 5), and every time the value of the variable x is displayed on the micro:bit LED screen and incremented by 2. **Table 7-1** shows how the output is calculated in each step.

Table 7-1. *Calculation steps of the 'for' loop*

Index	Print value of x	Calculation (x = x + 2)
0	0	0 + 2 = 2
1	2	2 + 2 = 4
2	4	4 + 2 = 6
3	6	6 + 2 = 8
4	8	8 + 2 = 10
5	10	Calculation stops

7-4. Decision Making with *if-then*

Problem

You want to display the **'yes'** icon on the micro:bit LED screen if the randomly generated number is **greater** than **5**.

Solution

- In the **Toolbox**, click the **Input** category and then click on the **on button A pressed** event block.

- In the **Toolbox**, click the **Variables** category. Then click on the **Make a Variable…** button. In the **New variable name** modal box, type **x**. Then click on the **Ok** button.

- In the **Toolbox**, click on the **Variables** category again. Then click and drag the **set *variable* to** block over, and place it inside the **on button A pressed** block. After that, choose the variable **x** from the drop-down list.

- In the **Toolbox**, click the **Math** category. Then click and drag the **pick random *0* to *10*** block over, and place it on the placeholder of the **set *x* to** block (**Figure 7-4**).

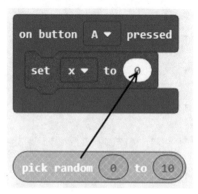

Figure 7-4. *Placing the **pick random** block*

- In the **Toolbox,** click on the **Logic** category. Then click and drag the **if-then** block over, and place it inside the **on button A pressed** block just below the **set *x* to** block.

- In the **Toolbox,** click on the **Logic** category again. Under the Comparison section, click and drag one of the **comparison** blocks over, and place it inside the placeholder of the **if-then** block. Choose > (**greater than**) from the drop-down list. Then click on the **Variables** category. Then click and drag the variable **x** over, and place it inside the first placeholder of the **comparison** block. Then type **5** in the second placeholder.

- Click on the **Basic** category. Then click and drag the **show icon** block over, and place it inside the **if-then** block. Choose the "**yes**" icon from the drop-down list if it has not already been selected. Also, drag and drop the **clear screen** block from the **Basic** category, and place it inside the **if-then** block just below the **show icon** block.

- Once completed, your code should look something like this (**Figure 7-5**).

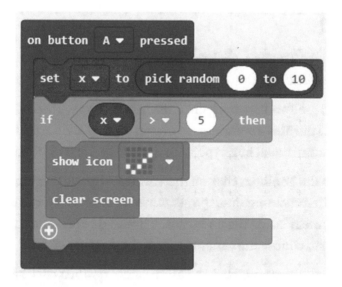

Figure 7-5. *Code listing*

How It Works

The **if-then** block allows you to identify if a certain condition is true or false and executes a block of code accordingly. In the above solution under Recipe 7-4, when you press the button **A**, a random number (0 to 10 between mix and max included) will assign to the variable **x**. Next, the if section of the **if-else** block is used to determine whether the variable **x** is greater than **5**. If *true*, the "**yes**" icon will display on the LED screen and then clear the screen to prepare it for the next event.

7-5. Decision Making with *If-then-else*

Problem

You want to display the '**yes**' icon on the micro:bit LED screen if the randomly generated number is *greater* than **5** and display the '**no**' icon if the randomly generated number is *less* than **5**.

Solution

- In the **Toolbox**, click the **Input** category, and then click on the **on button A pressed** event block.

- In the **Toolbox**, click the **Variables** category. Then click on the **Make a Variable…** button. In the **New variable name** modal box, type **x**. Then click on the **Ok** button.

- In the **Toolbox**, click on the **Variables** category again. Then click and drag the **set *variable* to** block over, and place it inside the **on button A pressed** block. After that, choose the variable **x** from the drop-down list.

- In the **Toolbox**, click the **Math** category. Then click and drag the **pick random *0* to *10*** block over, and place it on the placeholder of the **set *x* to** block (**Figure 7-6**).

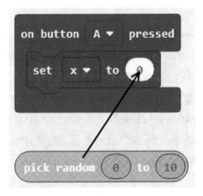

*Figure 7-6. Placing the **pick random** block*

- In the **Toolbox**, click on the **Logic** category. Then click and drag the **if-then-else** block over, and place it inside the **on button A pressed** block just below the **set *x* to** block.

- In the **Toolbox**, click on the **Logic** category again. Under the **Comparison** section, click and drag one of the **comparison** blocks over, and place it inside the placeholder of the **if-then** block. Choose > (**greater than**) from the drop-down list. Then click on the **Variables** category. Then click and drag the variable **x** over, and place it inside the first placeholder of the **comparison** block. Then type **5** in the second placeholder.

- Click on the **Basic** category. Then click and drag the **show icon** block over, and place it inside the **then** section of the **if-then-else** block. Choose the "**yes**" icon from the drop-down list. Also, drag and drop another **show icon** block from the **Basic** category, and place it inside the else section of the **if-then-else** block. Then choose the "**no**" icon from the drop-down list.

- Once completed, your code should look something like this (**Figure 7-7**).

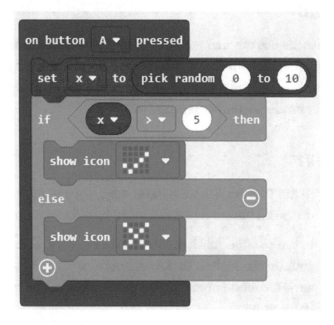

Figure 7-7. *Code listing*

155

How It Works

The **if-then-else** block allows you to identify if a certain condition is true or false and executes a block of code accordingly. In the above solution under Recipe 7-5, when you press the button **A**, a random number (0 to 10 between mix and max included) will assign to the variable **x**. Next, the **if** section of the **if-else** block is used to determine whether the variable **x** is *greater* than **5**. If **true**, the **then** section of the **if-then-else** will execute and display the "**yes**" icon on the LED screen. If the variable **x** is *less* than **5**, the block inside the **else** section will execute and the "**no**" icon will display on the LED screen.

7-6. Decision Making with *if-then-else if-then-else*

Problem

You want to display the **'yes'** icon on the micro:bit LED screen if the randomly generated number is *greater* than **5** and display the **'no'** icon if the randomly generated number is *less* than **5**. **Also, display the square icon, if the random number is equal to 5.**

Solution

- In the **Toolbox**, click the **Input** category, and then click on the **on button A pressed** event block.

- In the **Toolbox**, click the **Variables** category. Then click on the **Make a Variable...** button. In the **New variable name** modal box, type **x**. Then click on the **Ok** button.

- In the **Toolbox**, click on the **Variables** category again. Then click and drag the **set *variable* to** block over, and place it inside the **on button A pressed** block. After that, choose the variable **x** from the drop-down list.

- In the **Toolbox**, click the **Math** category. Then click and drag the **pick random *0* to *10*** block over, and place it on the placeholder of the **set *x* to** block (**Figure 7-8**).

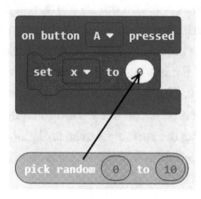

Figure 7-8. *Placing the **pick random** block*

- In the **Toolbox**, click on the **Logic** category. Then click and drag the **if-then-else** block over, and place it inside the **on button A pressed** block just below the **set *x* to** block. Click on the **plus** icon to add another section to the **if-then-else** block.

- In the **Toolbox**, click on the **Logic** category again. Under the **Comparison** section, click and drag one of the **comparison** blocks over, and place it inside the placeholder of the **if-then** block. Choose > (**greater than**) from the drop-down list. Then click on the

Variables category. Then click and drag the variable **x** over, and place it inside the first placeholder of the **comparison** block. Then type **5** in the second placeholder.

- Click on the **Basic** category. Then click and drag the **show icon** block over, and place it inside the **then** section of the **if-then-else** block. Choose the "**yes**" icon from the drop-down list.

- In the **Toolbox**, click on the **Logic** category. Under the **Comparison** section, click and drag one of the **comparison** blocks over, and place it inside the second placeholder if it belongs to the **else if** section of the **if-then** block. Choose < (**less than**) from the drop-down list. Then click on the **Variables** category. Then click and drag the variable **x** over, and place it inside the first placeholder of the **comparison** block. Then type **5** in the second placeholder.

- Also, drag and drop another **show icon** block from the **Basic** category, and place it inside the **else if** section of the **if-then-else** block. Then choose the "**no**" icon from the drop-down list.

- Finally, drag and drop one more **show icon** block from the **Basic** category, and place it inside the **else** section of the **if-then-else** block. Then choose "**square**" icon from the drop-down list.

- Once completed, your code should look something like this (**Figure 7-9**).

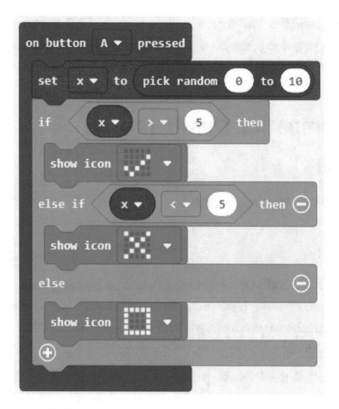

Figure 7-9. *Code listing*

How It Works

The **if-then-else** block allows you to identify if certain conditions are true or false and executes a block of code accordingly. In the above solution under Recipe 7-6, when you press the button **A**, a random number (0 to 10 between mix and max included) will assign to the variable **x**. Next, the **if** section of the **if-else** block is used to determine whether the variable **x** is *greater* than **5**. If **true**, the code block inside the first **then** section of the **if-then-else** block will execute and display the "**yes**" icon on the LED screen. If the variable **x** is *less* than **5**, the block inside the **else if** section will execute, and the "**no**" icon will display on the LED screen. If the variable **x** is *equal* to **5**, the block inside the **else** section will execute, and the "**square**" icon will display on the LED screen.

7-7. Comparing Numbers

Problem

You want to compare two numbers.

Solution

- In the **Toolbox**, click on the **Variables** category and then click on the **Make a Variable...** button. In the **New variable name** box, type **x**. Finally, click on the **Ok** button.

- Follow the above step again to make another variable named **y**.

- In the **Toolbox**, click on the **Variables** category. Then click and drag the **set y to** block over, and place it inside the **on start** block. Now right-click on the **set y to** block, and from the shortcut menu, choose **Duplicate**. Place the duplicated block just above the **set y to** block and choose the variable **x** from the drop-down list. Type the value **5** for both variables.

- In the **Toolbox**, click on the **Logic** category. Then click and drag the **if-then-else** block over and place it inside the **on start** block just below the **set y to** block.

- Click on the **Logic** category again. Under the **Comparison** section, click and drag one of the blocks over, and place it on the placeholder of the **if-then-else** block (by default, the placeholder has a **true-false** block). Then choose "**=**" from the drop-down list.

- Click on the **Variables** category. Then click and drag the variable **x** over and place it on the *first placeholder* of the **comparison** block. Also, click and drag the variable **y** block over, and place it on the *second placeholder* of the **comparison** block.

- Click on the **Basic** category. Then click and drag the **show icon** block over, and place it inside the *then* section of the **if-then-else** block. After that, choose the "**yes**" icon from the drop-down list.

- Follow the above step to place another **show icon** block inside the *else* section of the **if-then-else** block, and choose the "**no**" icon from the drop-down list.

- Once completed, your code should look something like this (**Figure 7-10**).

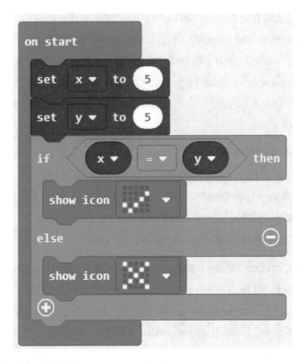

Figure 7-10. *Code listing*

How It Works

The comparison block allows you to compare two numbers (inputs).

- = Return true if both inputs equal each other.

- ≠ Return true if both inputs are not equal to each other.

- < Return true if the first input is smaller than the second input.

- ≤ Return true if the first input is smaller than or equal to the second input.

- > Return true if the first input is greater than the second input.

- ≥ Return true if the first input is greater than or equal to the second input.

7-8. Using Boolean Operators

Problem

You want to check if the user has pressed both buttons connected to the pin0 and pin1.

Solution

You will need following things to build the circuit.

- micro:bit
- Two toggle switches (https://www.sparkfun.com/products/9276)
- Two 10 kilo Ohm resistors
- Alligator leads

First, build the circuit as shown in **Figure 7-11**.

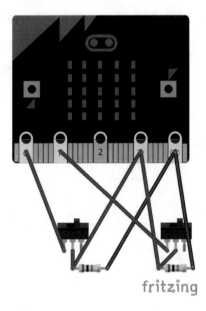

Figure 7-11. *Wiring diagram*

Then follow the steps below to build the code with MakeCode.

- In the **Toolbox**, click on the **Input** category and then click on the **on button A pressed** event block.

- In the **Toolbox**, click on the **Variables** category and then click on the **Make a Variable...** button. In the **New variable name** box, type **x**. Finally, click on the **Ok** button.

- Follow the above step again to make another variable named **y**.

- In the **Toolbox**, click on the **Variables** category. Then click and drag the **set y to** block over, and place it inside the **on button A pressed** block. Now right-click on the **set y to** block and from the shortcut menu, choose **Duplicate**. Place the duplicated block just above the **set y to** block and choose the variable **x** from the drop-down list.

- Click on the **Pins** category. Then click and drag the **digital read pin P0** block over, and place it inside the placeholder of the **set x to** block.

- Follow the above step to place another digital read pin P0 block inside the placeholder of the **set y to** block. Then choose the pin **P1** from the drop-down list.

- In the **Toolbox**, click on the **Logic** category. Then click and drag the **if-then-else** block over, and place it inside the **on start** block just below the **set y to** block.

- Click on the **Logic** category again. Under the **Boolean** section, click and drag the **Boolean and** block over, and place it on the placeholder of the **if-then-else** block (by default, the placeholder has a **true-false** block).

- Click on the **Variables** category. Then click and drag the variable **x** over, and place it on the *first placeholder* of the **comparison** block. Also, click and drag the variable **y** block over, and place it on the *second placeholder* of the **comparison** block.

- Click on the **Basic** category. Then click and drag the **show icon** block over, and place it inside the *then* section of the **if-then-else** block. After that, choose the **"yes"** icon from the drop-down list.

- Follow the above step to place another **show icon** block inside the *else* section of the **if-then-else** block, and choose the **"no"** icon from the drop-down list.

- Once completed, your code should look something like this (**Figure 7-12**).

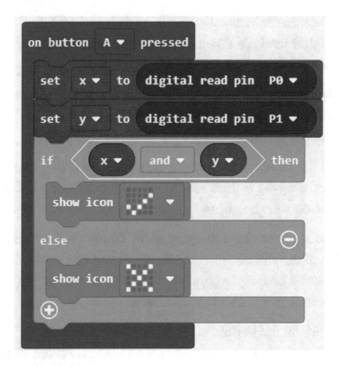

Figure 7-12. *Code listing*

How It Works

Boolean operators allow you to take Boolean inputs (true and false, 1 and 0) and evaluate to a Boolean output. MakeCode provides three Boolean operators:

- **And**: Evaluates to *true* **if-and-only-if** both inputs are *true*. **Table 7-2** shows the truth table for the Boolean **And**.

Table 7-2. *Truth table for **AND** operator*

Input A	Input B	Output
True	Ture	True
True	False	False
False	True	False
False	False	False

- **Or**: Evaluates to ***true* if-and-only-if** either input is ***true*. Table 7-3** shows the truth table for the Boolean operator **Or**.

Table 7-3. *Truth table for **OR** operator*

Input A	Input B	Output
True	Ture	True
True	False	True
False	True	True
False	False	False

- **Not**: Evaluates to the ***opposite*** of the input. **Table 7-4** shows the truth table for the Boolean operator **Not**.

Table 7-4. *Truth table for **NOT** operator*

Input	Output
True	False
False	True

In the above solution under Recipe 7-8, when you press the button A, the variables **x** and **y** take the status of the switches connected to the pin0 and pin1. The status of a switch can be either 1 or 0 (ON or OFF). Then the Boolean **And** operator evaluates to *true* if-and-only-if both inputs are 1 (both switches are turned ON). If true, the **'yes'** icon will display on the LED screen. If *false*, the **'no'** icon will display on the LED screen.

CHAPTER 8

Using Mathematical Functions

This chapter presents how to use the built-in mathematical functions to add, subtract, multiply, or divide numeric values; create pseudorandom numbers; find the absolute values of numbers; calculate the remainders; find max and min values; and convert ASCII characters to text.

8-1. Using Basic Mathematical Operations
Problem

You want to use basic mathematical operations such as addition, subtraction, multiplication, and quotient division with two numbers.

Solution

- In the **Toolbox**, click on the **Variables** category and then click on the **Make a Variable...** button. In the **New variable name** modal box, type **x** and click on the **Ok** button.

- Repeat the above step again to create another **variable** named **y**.

© Pradeeka Seneviratne 2019
P. Seneviratne, *BBC micro:bit Recipes*, https://doi.org/10.1007/978-1-4842-4913-0_8

- Again, click on the **Variables** category. Then click and drag the **set *variable* to** block over, and place it inside the **on start** block. Then choose the variable **x** from the drop-down list and type **8** in the text box.

- Repeat the above step to place another **set *variable* to** block just below the set **x** to block, and choose the variable **y** from the drop-down list and type **2** in the text box.

- In the **Toolbox,** click on the **Basic** category. Then click and drag the **show number** block over, and place it inside the **on start** block just below the **set *y* to** block.

- In the **Toolbox**, click on the **Math** category. Then click and drag the **addition** block over, and place it inside the **placeholder** of the **show number** block.

- In the **Toolbox**, click on the **Variables** category. Then click and drag the variable **x** over, and place it inside the *first* **placeholder** of the **addition** block.

- Repeat the above step again to place the variable **y** in the *second* **placeholder** of the **addition** block.

- Right-click on the **show number** block, and from the shortcut menu, click **Duplicate**. Then place it inside the **on start** block just below the first **show number** block. After that, choose **subtraction** from the drop-down list.

- Repeat the above step to create and place blocks for multiplication and quotient division.

- In the **Toolbox**, click on the **Basic** category. Then click and drag the **show string** block over, and place it just above the **addition** block. Type "**Addition**" in the text box of the **show string** block.

- Repeat the above step to create another three **show string** blocks for "**Subtraction**," "**Multiplication**," and "**Division**." Place them just above the respective mathematical operation blocks.

- Once completed, your code should look something like this (**Figure 8-1**).

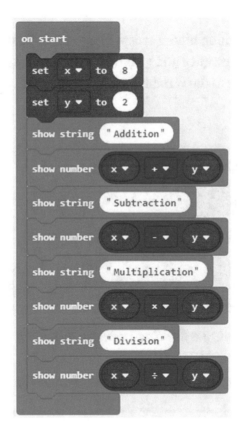

Figure 8-1. *Full code listing*

- After flashing the code, micro:bit will display the following result on the LED screen.

```
Addition: 10 Subtraction: 6 Multiplication: 16 Division: 4
```

How It Works

Mathematical operation blocks accept integers and floating-point numbers (includes positive and negative) as inputs. **Figure 8-2** shows how to assign −0.8 and 2 to the variables x and y, respectively, for calculating the sum.

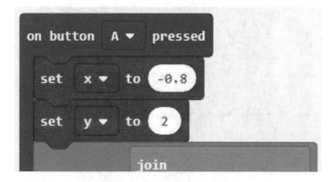

Figure 8-2. *Assigning a floating-point number to a variable*

The micro:bit will display following result on the LED screen.

```
1.2
```

8-2. Finding Smaller and Larger Values of Two Numbers

Problem

You want to find the smaller value of two numbers.

Solution

- In the **Toolbox**, click on the **Variables** category and then click on the **Make a Variable...** button. In the **New variable name** window, type **x** and click on the **Ok** button.

- Follow the above step again to create another **variable** named **y**.

- Again, go to the **Variables** category. Then click and drag the **set _variable_ to** block over, and place it inside the **on start** block. Then from the drop-down list, choose the **variable x** and in the text box, type the value **2**.

- Follow the above step again to place another **set _variable_ to** block just below the **set _x_ to** block. Then from the drop-down list, choose the **variable y** and in the text box, type the value **8**.

- In the **Toolbox**, click on the **Basic** category. Then click and drag the **show number** block over, and place it inside the **on start** block just below the **set _y_ to** block.

- In the **Toolbox**, click on the **Math** category. Then click and drag the **min of** block over, and place it inside the placeholder of the **show number** block.

- In the **Toolbox**, click on the **Variables** category. Then click and drag the **variable x** block over, and place it inside the *first placeholder* of the **min of** block.

- Follow the above step again to place the **variable y** in the *second* **placeholder** of the **min of** block.

- Once completed, your code should look something like this (**Figure 8-3**).

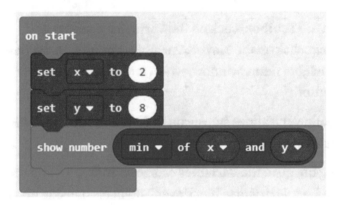

Figure 8-3. *Full code listing*

- When you run the code, the micro:bit display will show the following output.

2

How It Works

The **min of** block allows you to find the smaller value of two numbers. With the **min of** block, you can use variables, or you can type the values in the placeholders as inputs.

If you want to find the smaller value from more than two numbers, you can use a nested min of blocks. **Figure 8-4** shows the code to find the smaller value from the numbers **8, 2, 3,** and **5**. It has three nested **min of** blocks.

Figure 8-4. *Finding the smaller value from more than two numbers*

If you click on the drop-down box of the min block, you can choose the max option from the list. This will change the functionality of the block and can be used to find the larger value of two numbers. As an example, **Figure 8-5** shows how to find the larger value from two numbers.

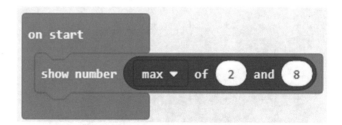

Figure 8-5. *Finding the larger value from two numbers*

The micro:bit display will show the following answer as the output.

8-3. Finding Absolute Value of a Number

Problem

You want to find the absolute value of a number.

Solution

- In the **Toolbox**, click on the **Basic** category. Then click and drag the **show number** block over, and place it inside the **on start** block.

- In the **Toolbox**, click on the **Math** category. Then click and drag the **absolute of** block over, and place it inside the placeholder of the **show number** block.

- Type the value **8** in the *text box* of the **absolute of** block.

- Once completed, your code should look something like this (**Figure 8-6**).

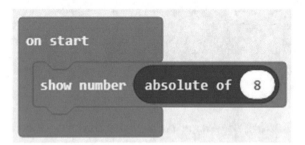

Figure 8-6. *Full code listing*

- When you run the code, micro:bit will display the following as the output.

8

How It Works

The absolute value tells only how far a number is from zero. As an example, "5" is **5** away from **zero**, and "−5" is also **5** away from **zero**. So, the absolute value of 5 is **5**, and the absolute value of −5 is also **5**.

Here are some more examples:

- The absolute value of −8 is **8**.

- The absolute value of 2 is **2**.

- The absolute value of 0 is **0**.

- The absolute value of −156 is **156**.

- The absolute value of 3.7 is **3.7**.

- The absolute value of −3.7 is **3.7**.

The absolute of block provides the absolute value of any number you have entered in the text box. It also accepts any number as a variable or number returned by another block.

8-4. Finding Square Root of a Number

Problem

You want to find the square root of a number.

Solution

- In the **Toolbox**, click on the **Basic** category. Then click and drag the **show number** block over. and place it inside the **on start** block.

- In the **Toolbox**, click on the **Math** category. Then click and drag the **square root** block over. and place it inside the placeholder of the **show number** block.

- Type the value **4** in the ***text box*** of the **square root** block.

- Once completed, your code should look something like this (**Figure 8-7**).

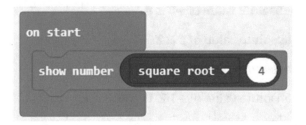

Figure 8-7. *Full code listing*

- When you run the code, the micro:bit displays the following as the output.

2

How It Works

The **square root** block outputs the square root of any positive number. It provides **NaN** (Not a Number) error message for any negative number, because negative numbers don't have a square root.

If you click on the drop-down list of the **square root** block, you can find a list of some useful mathematical functions. When you choose a function from the list, the name of the block will change and show the respective function name. They are the following:

- sin

- cos

- tan

- atan2

- integer ÷

- integer x

8-5. Rounding a Number

Problem

You want to round a number.

Solution

- In the **Toolbox**, click on the **Basic** category. Then click and drag the **show number** block over, and place it inside the **on start** block.

- In the **Toolbox**, click on the **Math** category. Then click and drag the **round** block over, and place it inside the placeholder of the **show number** block.

- Type the value **4.3** in the *text box* of the **round** block.

- Once completed, your code should look something like this (**Figure 8-8**).

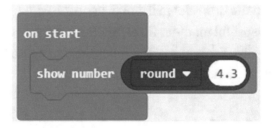

Figure 8-8. *Full code listing*

- When you run the code, the micro:bit displays the following as the output.

4

How It Works

The round block rounds any decimal number to the nearest whole number. Here are some examples:

Example: Round **2.4** to the nearest whole number.

Answer: **2**

(**2.4** gets **rounded down**)

Example: Round **2.7** to the nearest whole number.

Answer: **3**

(**2.7** gets **rounded up**)

Example: Round **2.5** to the nearest whole number.

Answer: **3**

(**2.5** gets **rounded up**)

Example: Round **2.48** to the nearest whole number.

Answer: **2**

(**2.48** gets **rounded down**)

Example: Round **2.59**

Answer: 3

(**2.59** gets **rounded up**)

8-6. Generating Random Numbers

Problem

You want to generate random numbers, including minimum and maximum numbers provided.

Solution

Let's generate random numbers between 5 and 12 included.

- In the **Toolbox**, click on the **Basic** category. Then click and drag the **show number** block over, and place it inside the **on start** block.

- In the **Toolbox**, click on the **Math** category. Then click and drag the **pick random** block over, and place it inside the placeholder of the **show number** block.

- Type **5** in the first text box of the pick random block as the minimum number.

- Type **12** in the second text box of the pick random block as the maximum number.

- Once completed, your code should look something like this (**Figure 8-9**).

```
on start
    show number  pick random  5  to  15
```

Figure 8-9. *Full code listing*

When you run the code, the micro:bit display shows one of the following numbers as the output.

5, 6, 7, 8, 9, 10, 11, 12, 13, 14, 15

How It Works

The **pick random** block outputs a random number between the minimum number and maximum number included. You can generate integers or decimal numbers, including negative and positive. Decimal numbers can be generated by providing at least one number for the minimum or maximum number.

The example below shows how to build a code to generate random numbers between **2.5** and **4.7** included (**Figure 8-10**).

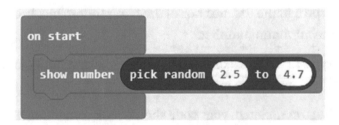

Figure 8-10. *Generating random numbers between two numbers*

Here are some output numbers generated by the above code. Note that some numbers have two decimal places, and some have one decimal place.

3.98, 2.64, 3.6, 3.91, 2.97, 4.44, 4.11.

8-7. Mapping a Number in One Range to Another Range

Problem

You want to map numbers in the range from 0–5 to another range from 0–1023.

Solution

- In the **Toolbox**, click on the **Basic** category. Then click and drag the **show number** block over, and place it inside the **on start** block.

- In the **Toolbox**, click on the **Math** category. Then click and drag the **map** block over, and place it inside the placeholder of the **show number** block.

- Type **2** in the first text box (map) as the voltage you want to map.

- Type **0** in the second text box (from low) as the minimum number of the range to convert from.

- Type **5** in the third text box (from high) as the maximum number of the range to convert from.

- Type **0** in the fourth text box (to low) as the minimum number of the range to convert to.

- Type **1023** in the fifth text box (to high) as the maximum number of the range to convert to.

- Once completed, your code should look something like this (**Figure 8-11**).

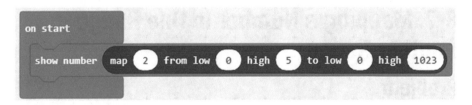

Figure 8-11. *Full code listing*

- When you run the above code, the micro:bit display shows the output as **409.2**.

How It Works

The map block converts a value in one number range to a value in another number range. Following are the parameters of the map block.

- **value**: a number to convert from one range to another.

- **from low**: the minimum number of the range to convert from.

- **from high**: the maximum number of the range to convert from.

- **to low**: the minimum number of the range to convert to.

- **to high**: the maximum number of the range to convert to.

As an example, you can scale a length in the range 0–10 cm to the range 0–100 cm. **Table 8-1** shows some mapped lengths from a small range to a large range.

Table 8-1. *Mapping Numbers from One Range to Another Range*

Length in range (0–10 cm)	Length in range (0–100 cm) after mapped
0	0
1	10
2	20
3	30
4	40
5	50
6	60
7	70
8	80
9	90
10	100

CHAPTER 9

Using Variables

This chapter presents how to create variables to hold various types of data such as numbers, strings, arrays, and Boolean values. It also presents how to take data out from the variables for further processing, and how to change data stored in the variables during the execution of the code.

9-1. Creating Integer Variables

Problem

You want to create a variable and store the value 100 in it, then display the content on the micro:bit display.

Solution

- In the **Toolbox**, click on the **Variables** category and then click the **Make a Variable...** button (**Figure 9-1**).

© Pradeeka Seneviratne 2019
P. Seneviratne, *BBC micro:bit Recipes*, https://doi.org/10.1007/978-1-4842-4913-0_9

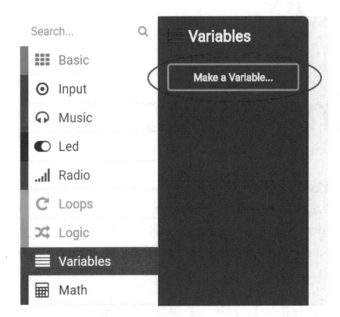

Figure 9-1. *The **Variables** toolbox*

- In the **New Variable name:** window, type **x** as the variable name. Then click on the **Ok** button (**Figure 9-2**).

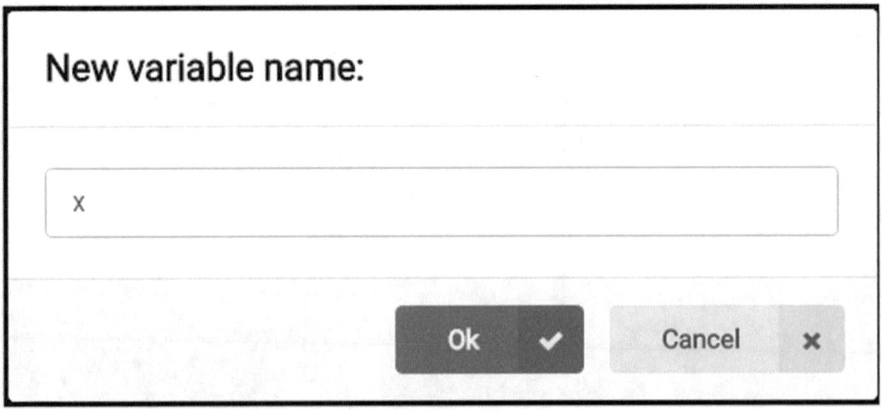

New variable name:

X

Ok ✔   Cancel ✕

Figure 9-2. *Creating a new variable*

- In the **Toolbox**, click on the **Variables** category again. Then click and drag the **set x to** block over, and place it inside the **on start** block (**Figure 9-3**).

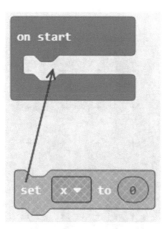

Figure 9-3. *Placing a **set variable to** block inside the **on start** block*

- Type the value **100** in the text box of the **set x to** block (**Figure 9-4**).

Figure 9-4. *Assigning a value to a variable*

- In the **Toolbox**, click the **Basic** category. Then click and drag the **show number** block over, and place it inside the **on start** block just below the **set x to** block.

- In the **Toolbox**, click the **Variables** category. Then click and drag the **variable x** block over, and place it inside the placeholder of the **show number** block (**Figure 9-5**).

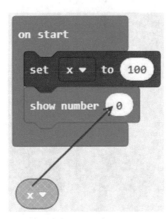

Figure 9-5. *Placing a **variable** into the **show number** block*

- Once completed, your code should look something like this (**Figure 9-6**).

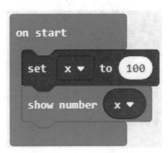

Figure 9-6. *Full code listing*

How It Works

When you create a variable, **MakeCode** doesn't know the *type* of the variable, until you first assign *data* to it. MakeCode supports the following standard **data types**:

- Number

- String

- Array

- Boolean

In the above example, the name of the variable **x** is known as the **operand**. When you store the number **100** as the **initial value** in the variable **x**, it will implicitly declare as an **integer** variable. MakeCode supports the following **numerical types**.

- int (includes signed and unsigned integers)

- float (including floating-point real values, signed and unsigned floating-point numbers)

Figure 9-7 shows how to assign a signed integer (negative integer value) to a variable by typing with a minus sign in front of it.

Figure 9-7. *Assigning a negative number to a variable*

9-2. Creating Float Variables

Problem

You want to create a variable and store the value 10.1 in it, then display the content on the micro:bit display.

Solution

- In the **Toolbox**, click on the **Variables** category and then click the **Make a Variable...** button (**Figure 9-8**).

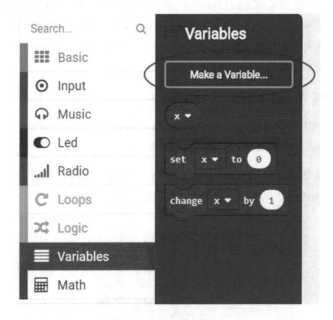

*Figure 9-8. The **Variables** toolbox*

- In the **New Variable name:** window, type **y** as the variable name. Then click on the **Ok** button (**Figure 9-9**).

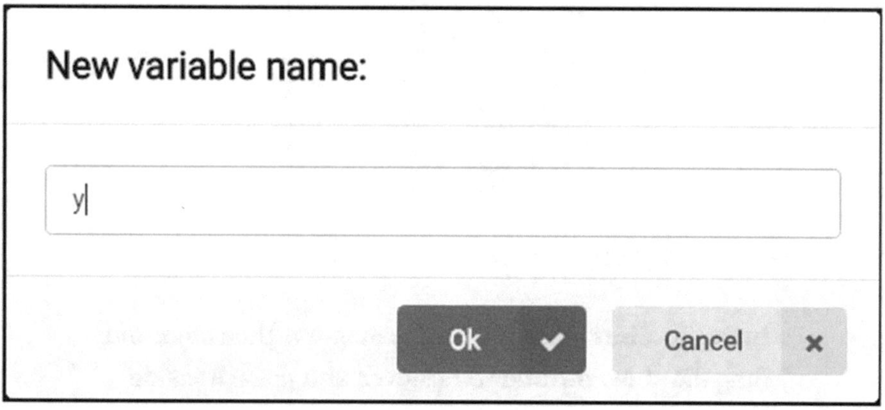

New variable name:

y|

Ok ✓   Cancel ✗

Figure 9-9. *Creating a variable*

- In the **Toolbox**, click on the **Variables** category again.
  Then click and drag the **set y to** block over, and place it
  inside the **on start** block (**Figure 9-10**).

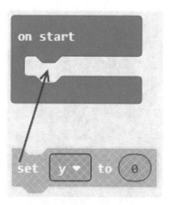

Figure 9-10. *Placing a **set variable to** block inside the **on start** block*

- Type the value **10.1** in the text box of the **set y to** block
  (**Figure 9-11**).

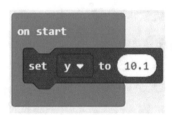

Figure 9-11. *Assigning a value to a variable*

- In the **Toolbox**, click the **Basic** category. Then click and drag the **show number** block over, and place it inside the **on start** block just below the **set y to** block.

- In the **Toolbox**, click the **Variables** category. Then click and drag the **variable y** block over, and place it inside the placeholder of the **show number** block (**Figure 9-12**).

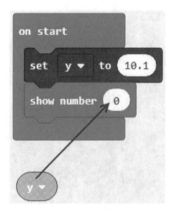

Figure 9-12. *Placing a **variable** into the **show number** block*

- Once completed, your code should look something like this (**Figure 9-13**).

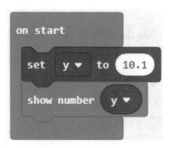

Figure 9-13. *Full code listing*

How It Works

Numbers created using a float variable declaration will have digits on both sides of a decimal point. When you first assign a decimal value to a variable, it will implicitly declare as a decimal variable. The decimal value could be unsigned or signed. **Figure 9-14** shows how to assign a signed decimal value (negative decimal value) to a variable by typing with a minus sign in front of.

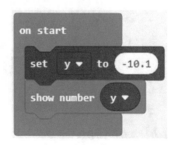

Figure 9-14. *Assigning a negative number to a variable*

9-3. Creating String Variables

Problem

You want to create a variable and store the string "micro:bit" in it, then display the content on the micro:bit display.

Solution

- In the **Toolbox**, click on the **Variables** category and then click the **Make a Variable...** button (**Figure 9-15**).

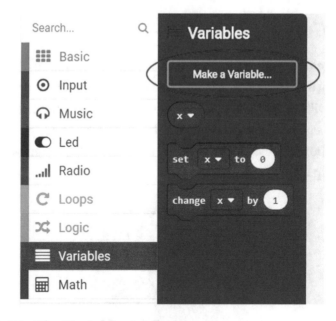

Figure 9-15. The Variables toolbox

- In the **New Variable name:** window, type **y** as the variable name. Then click on the **Ok** button (**Figure 9-16**).

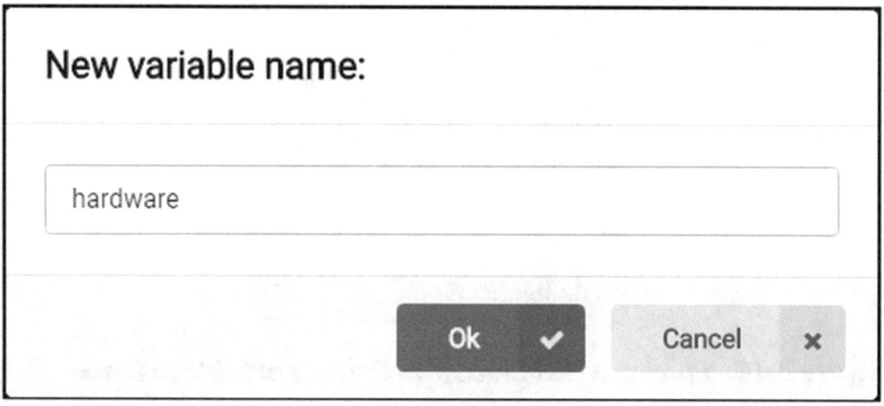

New variable name:

hardware

Ok ✓   Cancel ✗

Figure 9-16. Creating a variable name

- In the **Toolbox**, click on the **Variables** category again. Then click and drag the **set hardware to** block over, and place it inside the **on start** block (**Figure 9-17**).

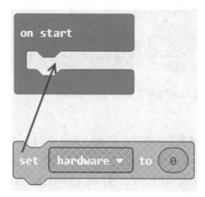

Figure 9-17. Placing a set variable to block inside the on start block

- In the **Toolbox**, click on the **Text** category. Then click and drag the **text** block over, and place it inside the placeholder of the **set hardware to** block (**Figure 9-18**).

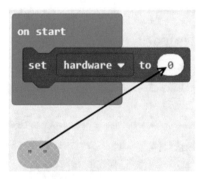

Figure 9-18. *Placing a **text** block into the **set variable to** block*

- Type the string **micro:bit** in the text block of the **set hardware to** block (**Figure 9-19**).

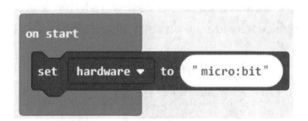

Figure 9-19. *Assigning a text to a variable*

- In the **Toolbox**, click the **Basic** category. Then click and drag the **show string** block over, and place it inside the **on start** block just below the **set hardware to** block.

- In the **Toolbox**, click the **Variables** category. Then click and drag the **variable hardware** block over, and place it inside the placeholder of the **show string** block (**Figure 9-20**).

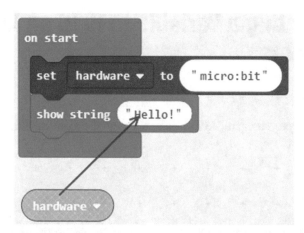

Figure 9-20. *Placing a variable into the **show string** block*

- Once completed, your code should look something like this (**Figure 9-21**).

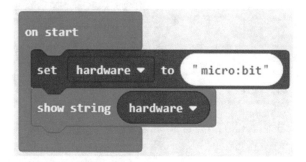

Figure 9-21. *Full code listing*

How It Works

By default, the **set variable to** block only accepts numbers and doesn't allow you to type strings in its **input box**. As a solution, you can replace the default input box with a **text** block from the **Text** category. This will allow the **set variable to** block to accept and hold any string.

9-4. Creating a Variable to Hold an Array of Numbers

Problem

You want to create a variable to hold an array of scores and find the score at index 4.

Solution

- In the **Toolbox**, click on the **Variables** category and then click the **Make a Variable...** button (**Figure 9-22**).

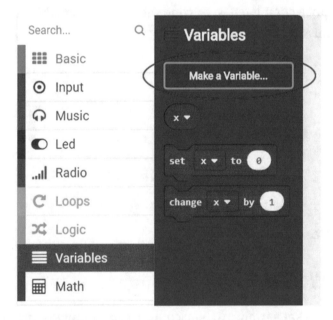

Figure 9-22. *The **Variables** toolbox*

- In the **New Variable name:** window, type **scores** as the variable name. Then click on the **Ok** button (**Figure 9-23**).

New variable name:

scores|

Ok ✔   Cancel ✖

Figure 9-23. *Creating a variable*

- In the **Toolbox**, click on the **Array** category. Then click and drag the **set list to** block over, and place it inside the **on start** block. The **set list to** block has an **array of** block that can hold numbers. By default, it has two number boxes for numeric inputs.

- Click on the drop-down box of the **set list to** block and from the drop-down list, choose the variable **scores**.

- Click on the + icon to add three more number boxes. Then type the scores in each number box (**2, 3, 0, 2, 1**) (**Figure 9-24**).

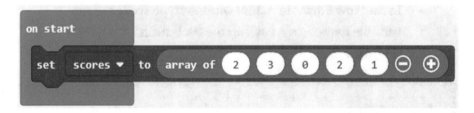

Figure 9-24. *Using the **array of** block*

- In the **Toolbox**, click on the **Basic** category. Then click
  and drag the **show number** block over, and place it
  inside the **on start** block just below the **set scores to**
  block.

- In the **Toolbox**, click on the **Arrays** category. Then
  click and drag the **get value at** block over, and place
  it inside the placeholder of the **show number** block
  (**Figure 9-25**).

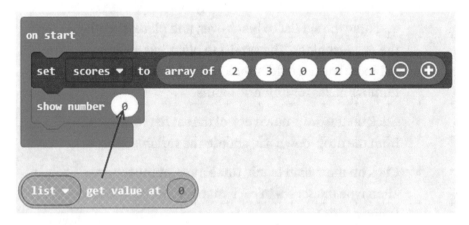

Figure 9-25. *Placing the **get value at** block*

- In the **get value at** block, choose the variable **scores**
  from the drop-down list. Then in the text box, type the
  index of the value you want to find (e.g., 4).

- Once completed, your code should look something like this (**Figure 9-26**).

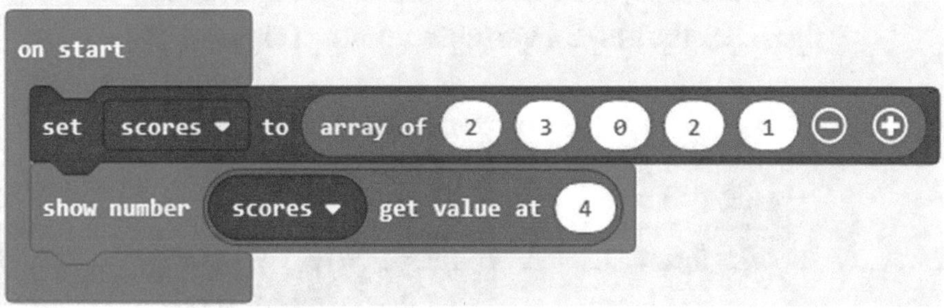

Figure 9-26.   Full code listing

How It Works

The **set list to** block allows you to store an array of numbers. Each number in the array has an index and starts from 0. In the above example, the first number, which is, 2 has the index 0. The last number, which is 1, has the index 4. The **get value at** block is used to find the value at any valid index. For the above example, the valid indexes are, 0, 1, 2, 3, and 4. The **show number** block is used to display the retrieved value on the micro:bit display.

9-5. Creating a Variable to Hold an Array of Text

Problem

You want to create a variable to hold an array of five names and find the name at index 4.

Solution

- In the **Toolbox**, click on the **Variables** category and then click the **Make a Variable...** button (**Figure 9-27**).

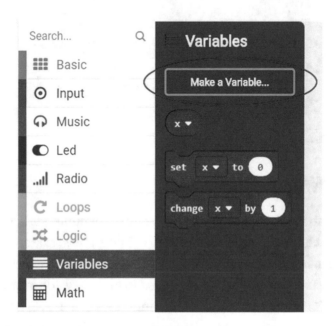

Figure 9-27. *The **Variables** toolbox*

- In the **New Variable name:** window, type **names** as the variable name. Then click on the **Ok** button (**Figure 9-28**).

Figure 9-28. *Creating a variable*

- In the **Toolbox**, click on the **Array** category. Then click and drag the **set text list to** block over, and place it inside the **on start** block. The **set text list to** block has an **array of** blocks that can hold strings. By default, it has two text boxes for inputs.

- Click on the drop-down box of the **set text list to** block and from the drop-down list, choose the variable **names**.

- Click on the + icon to add three more text boxes. Then type the names in each text box (**Emma, Olivia, Ava, Isabella, Sophia**) (**Figure 9-29**).

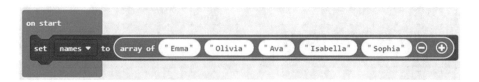

Figure 9-29.   *Using the* ***array of*** *block*

- In the **Toolbox**, click on the **Basic** category. Then click and drag the **show string** block over, and place it inside the **on start** block just below the **set names to** block.

- In the **Toolbox**, click on the **Arrays** category. Then click and drag the **get value at** block over, and place it inside the placeholder of the **show string** block (**Figure 9-30**).

Figure 9-30.   *Placing the* ***get value at*** *block*

- In the **get value at** block, choose the variable **names** from the drop-down list. Then in the text box, type the index of the **name** (string) you want to find (e.g., 4).

- Once completed your code should look something like this (**Figure 9-31**).

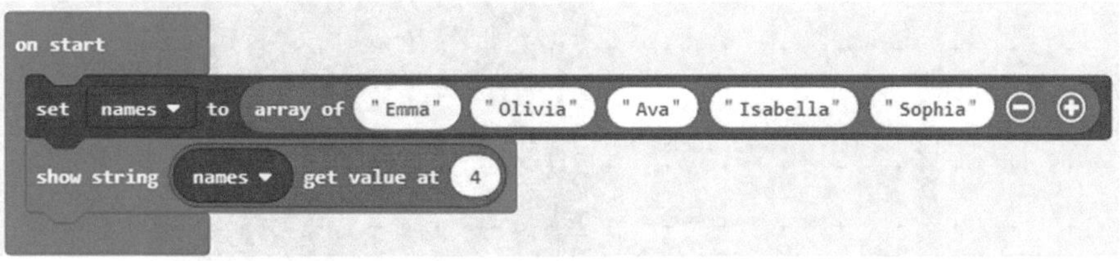

Figure 9-31. *Full code listing*

How It Works

The **set text list to** block allows you to store an array of strings. Each string in the array has an index and starts from 0. In the above example, the first number, which is 2, has the index 0. The last number, which is 1, has the index 4. The **get value at** bock is used to find the value at any valid index. For the above example, the valid indexes are, 0, 1, 2, 3, and 4. The show string block is used to display the retrieved string on the micro:bit display.

9-6. Creating a Variable to Hold Boolean Value

Problem

You want to create a variable to hold the value false.

Solution

- In the **Toolbox**, click on the **Variables** category and then click the **Make a Variable...** button (**Figure 9-32**).

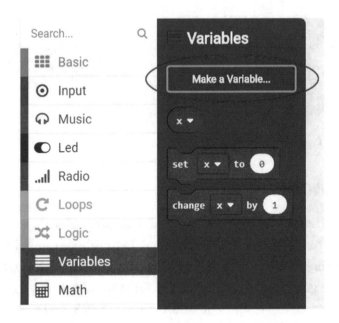

Figure 9-32. *The **Variables** toolbox*

- In the **New Variable name:** window, type **win**
  as the variable name. Then click on the **Ok** button
  (**Figure 9-33**).

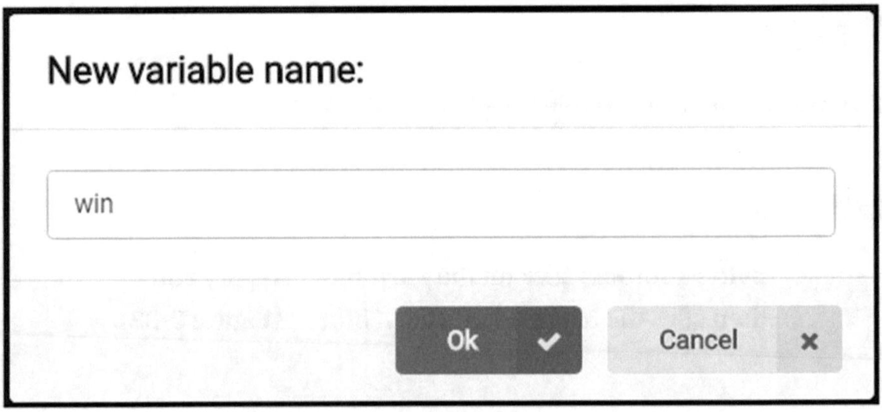

Figure 9-33. *Creating a variable*

- In the **Toolbox**, click on the **Variables** category. Then click and drag the **set variable to** block over, and place it inside the **on start** block. Then choose the variable **win** from the drop-down list.

- Click on the **Logic** category. Then click and drag the **Boolean false** block over, and place it inside the *placeholder* of the **set variable to** block (**Figure 9-34**).

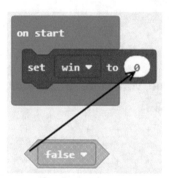

Figure 9-34. *Placing a **boolean** block*

- Click on the **Basic** category. Then click and drag the **show string** block over, and place it inside the **on start** block just below the **set win to** block.

- Click on the **Variables** category. Then click and drag the variable block named **win** over, and place it inside the placeholder of the **show string** block (**Figure 9-35**).

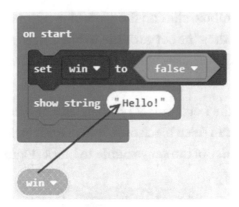

Figure 9-35. *Placing a variable*

- Once completed, your code should look something like this (**Figure 9-36**).

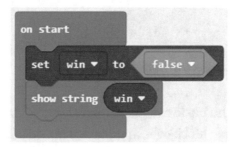

Figure 9-36. *Full code listing*

How It Works

MakeCode allows you to create variables that can hold two statuses: either true or false and known as Boolean variables. There are two Boolean blocks that can be found in the Logic category: true and false. You can choose either one and change the status by choosing true or false from the drop-down list.

9-7. Changing the Value of an Integer Variable

Problem

You want to change the value stored in the integer variable in **Recipe 9-1** by 10.

Solution

- Open the project you have created in **Recipe 9-1**.

- In the **Toolbox**, click on the **Variables** category. Then click and drag the **change variable by** block over, and place it inside the **on start** block just below the **show number** block.

- In the **change variable by** block, choose the variable **x** from the drop-down list. Then type the value **10** in the number box.

- Duplicate the **show number** block, and place it just below the **change x by** block. Then type **10** in the number box.

- Once completed, your code should look something like this (**Figure 9-37**).

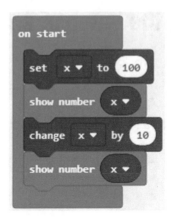

Figure 9-37. *Full code listing*

How It Works

Once assigned a value to an integer or float variable, you can change its value using one of the following ways.

- Use a **set variable to** block to assign a new value.

- Use a **change variable by** block to increment or decrement the current value by a specified value.

9-8. Updating String Variables

Problem

You want to change the content of the string variable created in **Recipe 9-3**.

Solution

- Open the code that you have created in **Recipe 9-3**.

- Duplicate the **set y to** block, and place the duplicated block just below the **show string** block. Then type **Calliope Mini** in the text box.

- Duplicate the **show string** block, and place the duplicated block just below the second **set y to** block.

- Once completed, your code should look something like this (**Figure 9-38**).

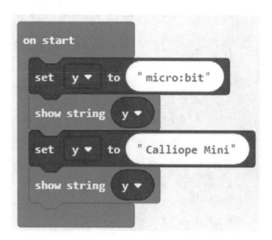

Figure 9-38. *Full code listing*

How It Works

By storing text in a string variable, you can change its content by using a **set variable to** block. You can also store numbers but make MakeCode treat them as just text and not used for mathematical calculations unless you first convert them to numbers using a **parse to number** block.

CHAPTER 10

Functions and Arrays

First, this chapter presents how to create **functions** and use them in your code to reduce the coding time and debugging time. It also increases the readability of code and will make your code cleaner and more concise. Then it presents how to create different type of **arrays** and offer some useful functions that can be applied to arrays such as finding the number of items, replacing items, inserting items, removing items, finding the index of an item, traversing through arrays, and reversing arrays.

10-1. Creating a Function
Problem

You want to convert 12 inches to centimeters and display the result on the micro:bit screen.

Solution

- In the **Toolbox** click **Functions**. Then click on the **Make a Function**... button (**Figure 10-1**).

© Pradeeka Seneviratne 2019
P. Seneviratne, *BBC micro:bit Recipes*, https://doi.org/10.1007/978-1-4842-4913-0_10

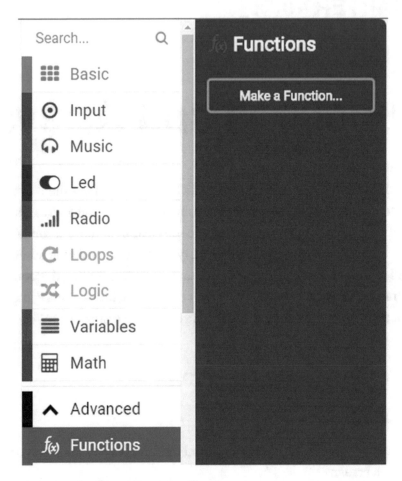

Figure 10-1. *The Functions toolbox*

- In the **New function name** window, type **inchesToCentimeters** as the function name. Then click on the **Ok** button (**Figure 10-2**).

New function name:

inchesToCentimeters

Ok ✓   Cancel ✗

Figure 10-2. *Creating a function name*

- The function block for **inchesToCentimeters** will add to the code area (**Figure 10-3**).

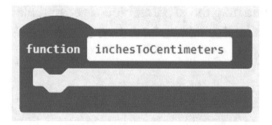

Figure 10-3. *A function block*

- In the **Toolbox**, click **Variables**. Then click on the **Make a Variable...** button.

- In the **New variable name...** window, type **inches** as the variable name. Then click on the **Ok** button.

- Repeat the above two steps to create the variable **centimeters**.

- In the **Toolbox**, click the **Variables** category. Then click and drag the **set variable to** block over, and place it inside the **function** block. Then choose the variable **centimeters** from the drop-down list (**Figure 10-4**).

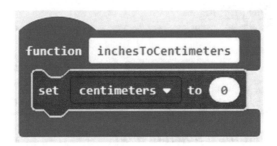

Figure 10-4. *Building the function*

- In the **Toolbox**, click on the **Math** category. Then click and drag the **division** block over, and place it inside the *placeholder* of the **set centimeters to** block (**Figure 10-5**).

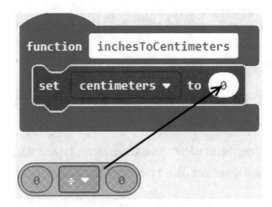

Figure 10-5. *Placing the **division** block*

- In the **Toolbox**, click on the **Variables** category. Then click and drag the **inches** variable block over, and place it inside the *left-side value box* of the **division** block (**Figure 10-6**).

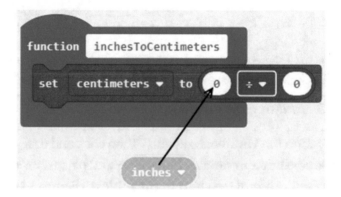

Figure 10-6. *Placing the **inches** variable*

- Type **0.3937** in the *right-side value box* of the **division** block (**Figure 10-7**).

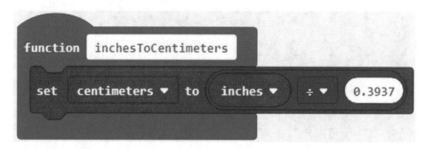

Figure 10-7. *Building the function*

- In the **Toolbox**, click on the **Basic** category. Then click and drag the **show number** block over, and place it inside the **function** block just below the **set centimeters to** block (**Figure 10-8**).

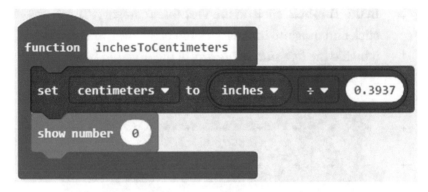

Figure 10-8. *Building the function*

- Click on the **Variables** category. Then click and drag the **centimeters** variable block over, and place it inside the *value box* of the **show number** block (**Figure 10-9**).

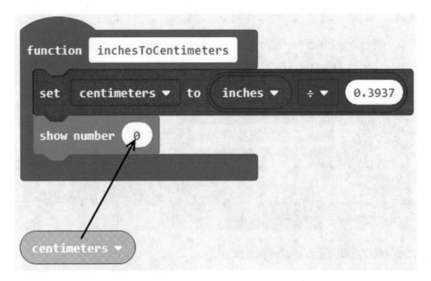

Figure 10-9. *Building the function*

- In the **Toolbox**, click on the **Variables** category. Next, click and drag the **set variable to** block over, and place it inside the **on start** block. After that, choose the variable **inches** from the drop-down list. Then type **12** in the *value box* (**Figure 10-10**).

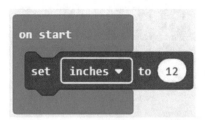

Figure 10-10. *Assigning a **number** to the **inches** variable*

- In the **Toolbox**, click on the **Functions** category. Next, click and drag the **call function** block over, and place it inside the **on start** block underneath the **set inches to** block. Then select **inchesToCentimeters** from the drop-down list (**Figure 10-11**).

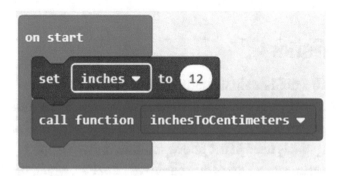

Figure 10-11. *Calling the function*

- Once completed, your code should look something like this (**Figure 10-12**).

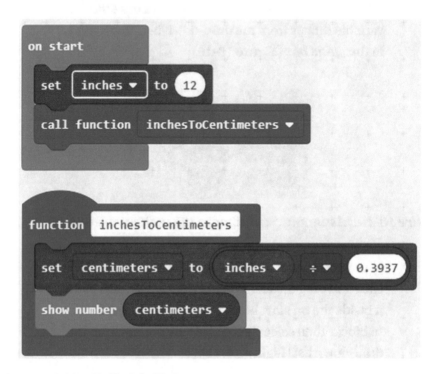

Figure 10-12. *Full code listing*

How It Works

Functions are a fundamental building block of your code. They allow you to create blocks of code that can be reused anywhere in the code.

Functions can accept data to process. These are known as parameters. The function that is used in the above solution under Recipe 10-1, **inchesToCentimeters()** takes one parameter, **inches**, which the function then uses to work out the value in centimeters. Some functions don't require parameters; an example of such would be a function that has been created to display a greeting on the screen.

In the above solution under Recipe 10-1, the function **inchesToCentimeters** contains the code to calculate inches into centimeters by dividing the inches by 0.3937. The calculated result is stored in the variable **centimeters**.

Before you call a function, first pass arguments for each parameter. In the above solution under Recipe 10-1, the argument **12** is passed to the parameter **inches** inside the **on start** block. Then you can call the function.

Figure 10-13 show how to reuse a function to calculate the area of some rectangles and squares in a code. First write a function (e.g., calculateArea) to calculate the area and store the calculated area in a variable (e.g., area). Then you can reuse the function by first assigning values to the parameters (e.g., x and y). Then call the function to execute the hidden code inside. The function will store the calculated area in a variable (e.g., area). Now you can print the calculated value stored in the variable using the **show number** block. The same function can be called to calculate the area of other rectangles and squares by following the same procedure.

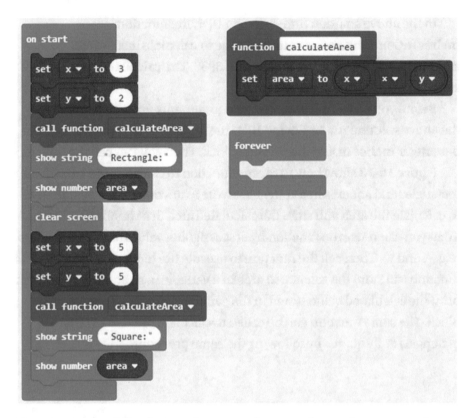

Figure 10-13. *Calculating the area of rectangles and squares using the same function*

10-2. Finding the Number of Items in an Array

Problem

You want to find the number of items in a number array and display the result on the micro:bit LED screen.

Solution

- In the **Toolbox**, click on the **Arrays** category. Then click and drag the **set list to** block over, and place it inside the **on start** block. By default, the **set list to** block holds a number array (**array of** block) with two items. When you drop the **set list to** block onto the code area, the variable, named **list** will create automatically.

- Add five items to the *array of* block; 2, 4, 6, 8, and 10. First replace the default values of two number boxes with 2 and 4, respectively. After that, use the *plus* icon to add three more number boxes. Then type the remaining numbers, 6, 8, and 10, respectively (**Figure 10-14**).

The **Array** *category* can be found in the **Toolbox** by expanding the **Advanced** *group*.

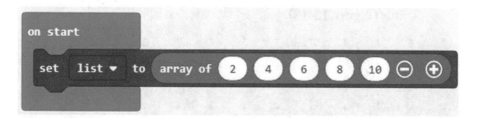

Figure 10-14. *Assigning an array to a variable*

- Click on the **Basic** category. Then click and drag the **show number** block over, and place it inside the **on start** block just below the **set list to** block.

225

- Click on the **Arrays** category again. Then click and drag the **length of array** block over, and place it inside the placeholder of the **show number** block (**Figure 10-15**). In the **length of array** block, choose **list** as the variable that holds the number array.

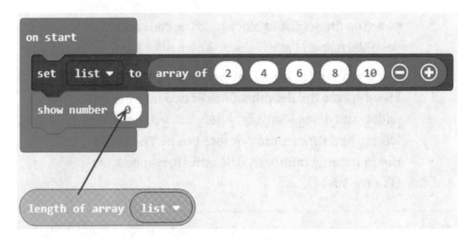

Figure 10-15. *Placing the **length of array** block*

- Once completed, your code should look something like this (**Figure 10-16**).

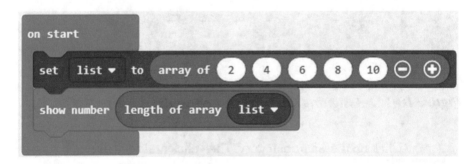

Figure 10-16. *Full code listing*

How It Works

The **length of array** block can be used to find the number of items in an array. It can be used with the number arrays as well as the string arrays.

An array can have zero items known as an 'empty array'.

In the above solution under Recipe 10-2, the number array is assigned to the variable named **list**. Then the **length of array** block is used to find the number of items in the array. Finally, the **show number** block is used to display the result on the LED screen. The **show string** block should also work.

Output: 5

10-3. Finding an Item at Specified Location in an Array

Problem

You want to find the item at index (position) 3 in a number array.

Solution

- Use the number array named **list** that you created in **Recipe 10-2 (Figure 10-17)**.

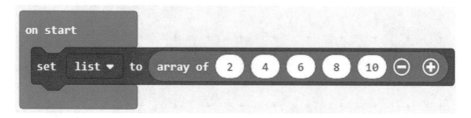

Figure 10-17. *Assigning a number array to a variable*

- In the **Toolbox**, click on the **Basic** category. Then click and drag the **show number** block over, and place it inside the **on start** block just below the **set list to** block.

- In the **Toolbox**, click on the **Arrays** category. Next, click and drag the **get value at** block over, and place it inside the *placeholder* of the **show number** block (**Figure 10-18**). After that, make sure to choose the variable **list** from the drop-down menu. Then type **3** in the number box for the position of the item.

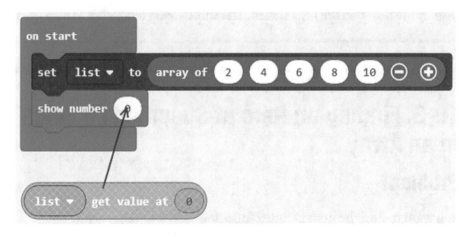

***Figure 10-18.** Placing the **get value at** block*

- Once completed, your code should look like this (**Figure 10-19**).

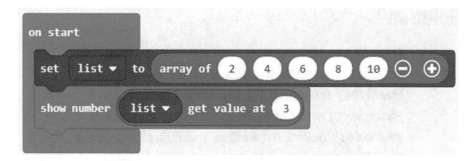

Figure 10-19. *Full code listing*

How It Works

The **get value at** block can be used to find any value at a specified index (position) in an array. The index starts from 0. The first item of an array has the index 0, the second item has the index 1, and so on. Likewise, the last item of an array has the index (number of items −1).

In the above solution under Recipe 10-3, the variable named **list** holds a number array that has five items. Then, the **get value at** block is used to find the item at index (position) **3**, which is **8**. Finally, the **show number** block is used to display the output on the LED screen.

When you run the code, you will get the following output.

8

The same thing can be applied to find an item in a **string array**. Just place the **get value at** block in the *placeholder* of the **show string** block.

10-4. Replacing an Item in an Array

Problem

You want to replace the item at index 2 with the letter 'd' in a string array. Then display the new item on the micro:bit LED screen.

Solution

- Click on the **Arrays** category. Then click and drag the **set text list to** block over, and place it inside the **on start** block. By default, the **set text list to** block has a **string array** with three items. When you add the **set text list to** block onto the editor, a variable named **text list** will create automatically.

- Click on the **Arrays** category again. Next, click and drag the **set value at** block over, and place it inside the **on start** block just below the **set text list to** block. After that, make sure to choose the variable **text list** from the drop-down menu. Then type **2** in the value box.

- Click on the **Text** category. Next, click and drag the **text box** block over, and place it inside the second placeholder of the **set value at** block. Then type the letter **d** in the text box (**Figure 10-20**).

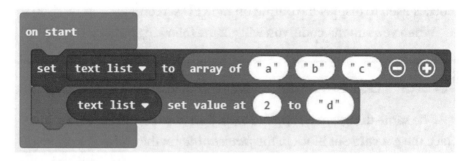

Figure 10-20. *Replacing an item in an array*

- Click on the **Basic** category. Then click and drag the **show string** block over, and place it inside the **on start** block.

- Click on the **Arrays** category. Next, click and drag the **get value at** block over, and place it inside the placeholder of the **show string** block. Then type *2* in the value box (**Figure 10-21**).

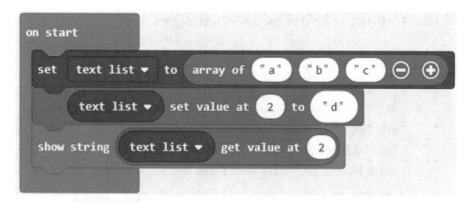

Figure 10-21. *Replacing an item in an array followed by verifying*

How It Works

The **set value at** block can be used to replace a value in an array at a specified index. In the above solution under Recipe 10-4, initially the index 2 holds the letter **c**. Next, the **set value at** block is used to replace the letter **c** with the letter **d**. After that, the **get value at** block is used to get the updated value at index 2. Then the **show string** block is used to display the returned value from the **get value at** block on the micro:bit LED screen.

When you run the code, you will get the following output.

d

10-5. Inserting an Item to the End of an Array

Problem

You want to insert an item to the end of a string array.

Solution

- In the **Toolbox**, click on the **Arrays** category. Then click and drag the **set text list to** block over, and place it inside the **on start** block. By default, the **set text list to** block has a string array with three items.

- Click on the **Arrays** category again. Then click and drag the **add value to end** block over, and place it inside the **on start** block just below the **set list to** block. Make sure to choose the variable **text list** from the drop-down menu.

- In the Toolbox, click on the **Text** category. Then click and drag the **text box** block over, and place it inside the *placeholder* of the **set value to end** block. Now type the letter **d** in the text box for the new item (**Figure 10-22**).

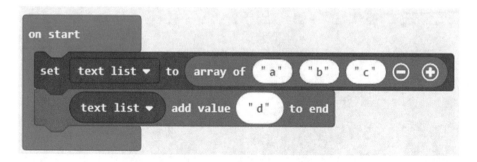

Figure 10-22. *Inserting an item to the end of an array*

- In the **Toolbox**, click on the **Basic** category. Then click and drag the **show string block** over, and place it inside the **on start** block just below the **add value to end** block.

- In the **Toolbox**, click on the **Arrays** category. Now, click and drag the **get value at** block over, and place it inside the placeholder of the show string block. After that, choose the variable **text list** from the drop-down menu. Then type **3** in the value box.

- Once completed, your code should look like the following (**Figure 10-23**).

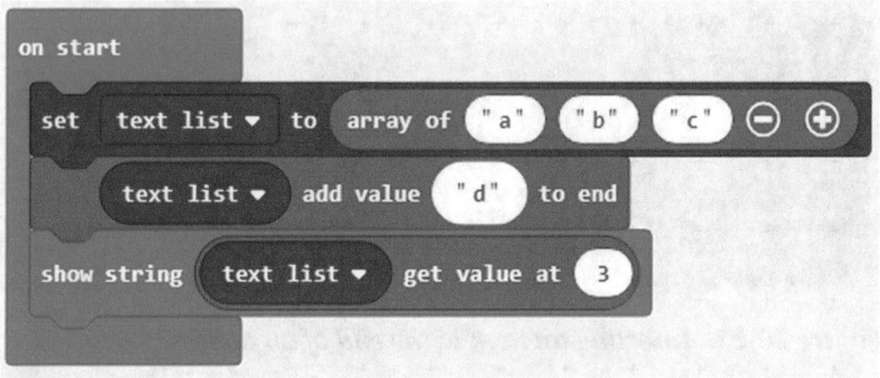

Figure 10-23. *Inserting an item to the end of an array followed by verifying*

How It Works

The **add value to end** block allows you to add a new item to the **end** of an array. In the above solution under Recipe 10-5, initially, the **string array** had three items. Next, the string **'d'** is added to the end of the string array using the **add value to end** block. After added, the resulting array has four items. Finally, the last item is displayed by combining the **show string** and **get value at** block.

When you run the code, you will get the following output.

---

d

In the same way, you can insert an item at **beginning** of an array using the **insert at beginning** block.

10-6. Removing Last Item from an Array

Problem

You want to get and remove the last item of a string array. Then display the removed item, followed by a new last item, followed by the number of items on the micro:bit display.

Solution

- In the **Toolbox**, click on the **Arrays** category. Then click and drag the **set text list to** block over, and place it inside the **on start** block. By default, the **set text list to** block has a string array with three items. When you add the **set text list to** block onto the code area, a variable named **text list** will create automatically.

- In the **Toolbox**, click on the **Basic** category. Then click and drag the **show string** block over, and place it inside the **on start** block just below the **set text list to** block.

- In the **Toolbox**, click on the **Arrays** category. Then click and drag the **get and remove last value from** block over, and place it inside the placeholder of the **show string** block. Choose the variable **text list** from the drop-down menu (**Figure 10-24**).

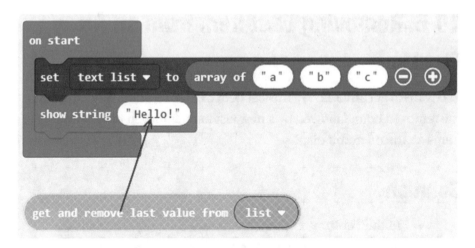

Figure 10-24. *Removing an item from an array*

- Click on the **Basic** category. Then click and drag the **show string** block over, and place it inside the **on start** block just below the **get and remove last value from** block.

- Click on the **Arrays** category. Then click and drag the **get value at block** over, and place it inside the placeholder of the **show string** block. Then type **1** in the value box.

- In the **Toolbox**, click on the **Basic** category. Then click and drag the **show number** block over, and place it inside the **on start** block just below the **show string** block.

- In the **Toolbox**, click on the **Arrays** category. Then click and drag the **length of array** block over, and place it inside the placeholder of the **show number** block. Choose the variable **text list** from the drop-down menu.

- Once completed, your code should look like the following (**Figure 10-25**).

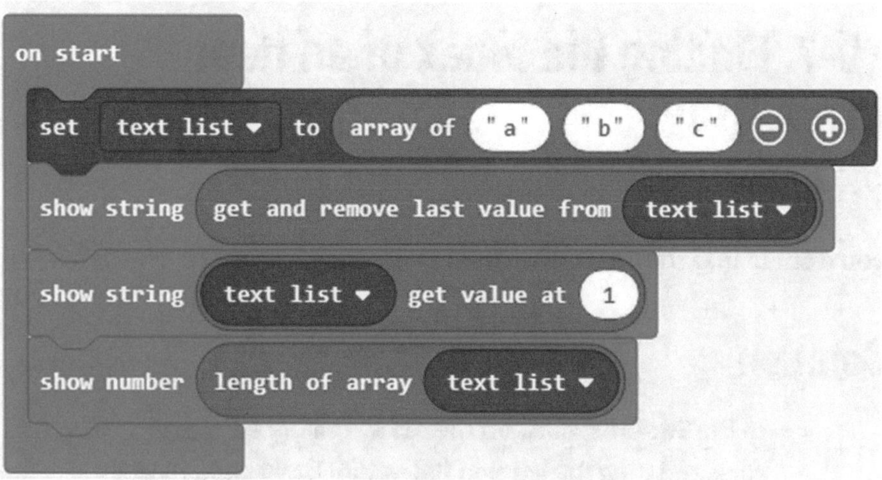

Figure 10-25. Full code listing

How It Works

The **get and remove last value from** block allows you to find the ***last item*** in an array and remove it from the list.

In the above solution under Recipe 10-6, initially, the string array had three items (a, b, c). First, the **get and remove last value from** block is used to get and remove the last item of the string array, which is the letter **'c'** at index 2. Then the removed item is displayed using the **show string** block. Once removed, the (new) last item is found using the **get value at block** and displayed using the **show string** block, which is the letter **'b'** at index 1. Next, we verified the number of items using the **length of array** block. When you run the code, you will get the following output.

c b 2

In the same way, you can use the **get and remove first** value from block to remove the *first item* from an array.

10-7. Finding the Index of an Item in an Array

Problem

You want to find the index of an item in an array.

Solution

- In the **Toolbox**, click on the **Arrays** category. Next, click and drag the **set text list to** block over, and place it inside the **on start** block. By default, the **set text list to** block has a string array with three items (a, b, c). Then click on the **plus** button to add two more text boxes and type **a** and **b**, respectively, in that text boxes. Now you should have a string array with five items.

- In the **Toolbox**, click on the **Basic** category. Then click and drag the **show number** block over, and place it inside the **on start** block just below the **set text list to** block.

- Click on the **Arrays** category. Click and drag the **find index of** block over, and place it inside the *placeholder* of the **show number** block.

- Click on the **Text** category. Then click and drag the **text box** block over, and place it inside the *placeholder* of the **find index of** block. Now type the letter **'b'** in the text box.

- Once completed, your code should look like the following (**Figure 10-26**).

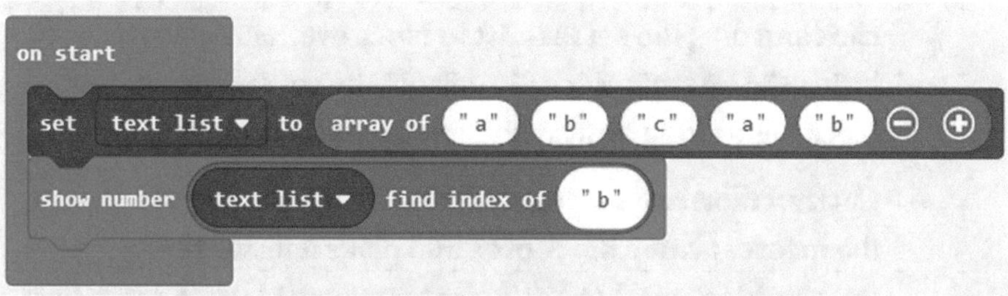

Figure 10-26. *Finding the index of an item in an array*

How It Works

The **find index of** block allows you to find the index of an item in an array. Remember, it can only be used to find the first occurrence from the start of an array for the given item.

In above solution under Recipe 10-9, the **find index of** block captured the index of the first occurrence of the letter **b**, which is 1. The show number block is used to display the output on the LED screen. When you run the code, you will get the following output.

1

If you try to find an element that is not existing in the array, micro:bit shows −**1** as the output.

10-8. Inserting an Item to an Array

Problem

You want to insert the letter z at index 1 of a string array with three items, a, b, and c. Then display the recently inserted item and number of items in the updated array.

Solution

- In the **Toolbox,** click on the **Arrays** category. Then click and drag the **set text list to** block over, and place it inside the **on start** block. By default, the **set text list to** block has a string array with three items (a, b, c).

- Click on the **Arrays** category again. Next, click and drag the **insert at value** block over, and place it inside the **on start** block just below the **set text list to** block. After that, the variable **text list** from the drop-down menu. Then type index **1** in the value box.

- Click on the **Text** category. Then click and drag the **text box** block over, and place it inside the *second placeholder* of the **insert at value** block. Then type the letter **z** in the text box (**Figure 10-27**).

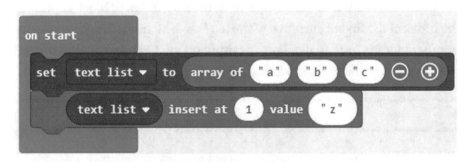

Figure 10-27. *Inserting an item to an array*

- Click on the **Basic** category. Then click and drag the **show string** block over, and place it inside the **on start** block just below the **insert at value** block.

- Click on the **Arrays** category. Next, click and drag the **get value at** block, and place it inside the *placeholder* of the **show string** block. After that, choose the variable **text list** from the drop-down menu. Then type index **1** in the value box (**Figure 10-28**).

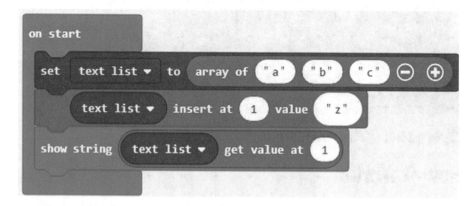

Figure 10-28. *Inserting an item to an array followed by verifying*

- Click on the **Basic** category. Then click and drag the **show number** block over, and place it inside the **on start** block just below the **show string** block.

- In the **Toolbox,** click on the **Arrays** category. Then click and drag the **length of array** block over, and place it inside the *placeholder* of the **show number** block. Choose the variable **text list** from the drop-down menu.

- Once completed, your code should look like the following (**Figure 10-29**).

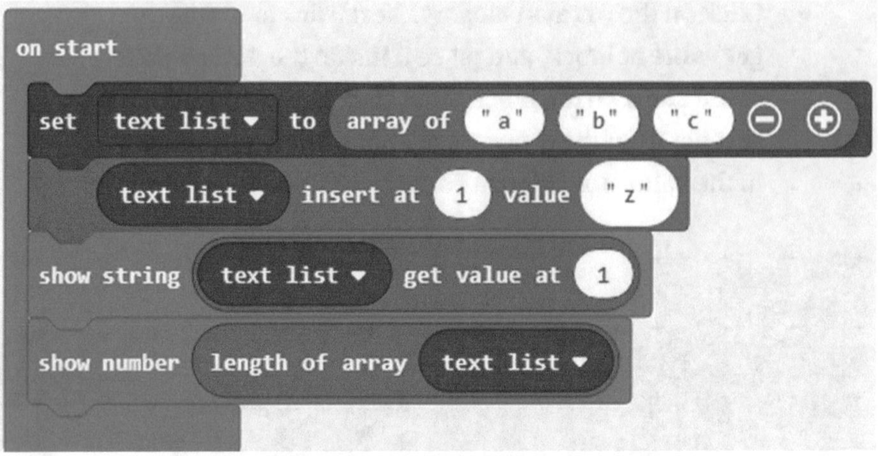

Figure 10-29. Full code listing

How It Works

The **insert at value** block allows you to insert an item to an array at the specified index (position). You can use it with any number array or string array.

In the above solution under Recipe 10-8, initially the string array had three items, a, b, and c. Then the **insert at value** block is used to insert item **z** at index **1**. When you run the code, you will get the following output.

---

z 4

10-9. Displaying All the Items of an Array

Problem

You want to display all the items in an array on the micro:bit LED screen.

Solution

- In the **Toolbox,** click on the **Arrays** category. Then click and drag the **set text list to** block over, and place it inside the **on start** block. By default, the **set text list to** block has a string array with three items (a, b, c). When you add the **set text list to** block onto the code area, a variable named **text list** will create automatically.

- Click on the **Loops** category. Next click and drag the **for element** block over, and place it inside the **on start** block just below the **set text list to** block. Then choose the variable **text list** from the drop-down menu.

- Click on the **Basic** category. Then click and drag the **show string** block over, and place it inside the **for element** block.

- Click on the **Variables** category. Then click and drag the **value** block over, and place it inside the *placeholder* of the **show string** block.

- Once completed, your code should look like the following (**Figure 10-30**).

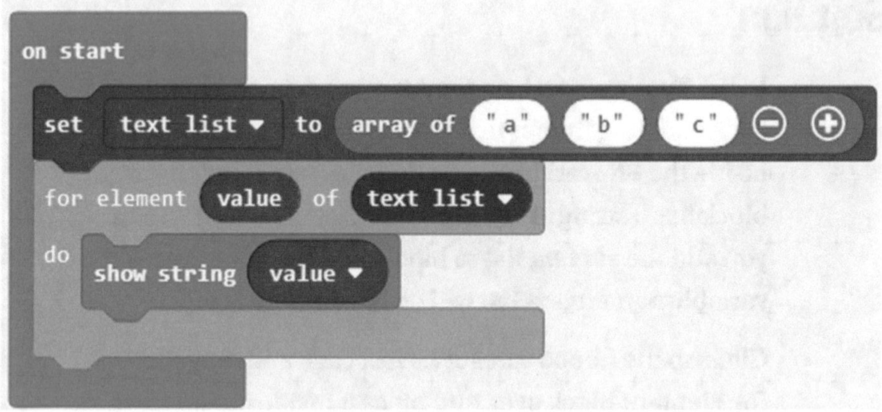

Figure 10-30. *Full code listing*

How It Works

Initially the array had three elements in the following sequence: a, b, c. Then the **for element** block is used to traverse through each item and display on the micro:bit LED screen using the **show string** block.

When you run the solution provided under Recipe 10-9, you will get the following output.

---

a b c

10-10. Reversing the Items of an Array

Problem

You want to reverse the items in an array and display them.

Solution

- In the **Toolbox,** click on the **Arrays** category. Then click and drag the **set text list to** block over, and place it inside the **on start** block. By default, the **set text list to** block has a string array with three items (a, b, c). When you add the set text list to block onto the code area, a variable named **text list** will create automatically.

- In the **Toolbox**, click on the **Arrays** category again. Next, click and drag the **reverse** block over, and place it inside the **on start** block just below the **set text list to** block. Then choose the variable **text list** from the drop-down menu.

- Click on the **Loops** category. Next, click and drag the **for element** block over, and place it inside the **on start** block just below the **reverse** block. Then choose the variable **text list** from the drop-down menu.

- Click on the **Basic** category. Then click and drag the **show string** block over, and place it inside the **for element** block.

- Click on the **Variables** category. Then click and drag the **value** block over, and place it inside the *placeholder* of the **show string** block.

- Once completed, your code should look like the following (**Figure 10-31**).

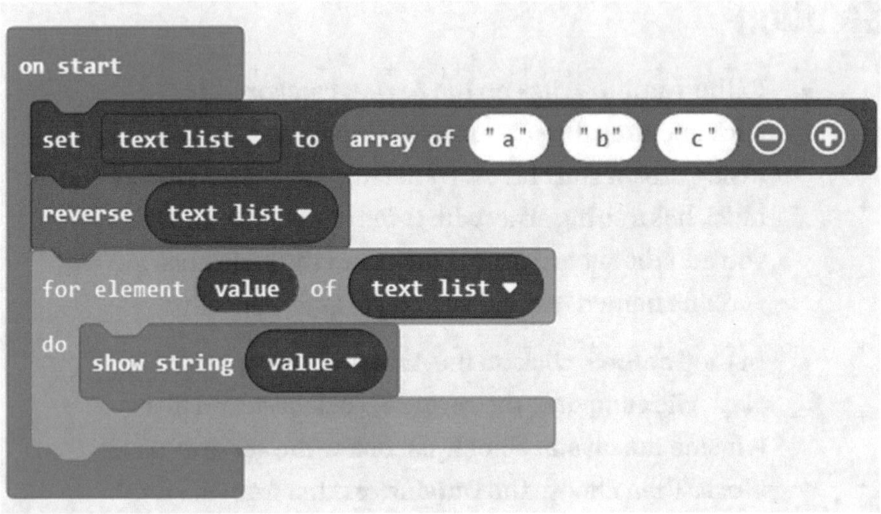

Figure 10-31. *Full code listing*

How It Works

The reverse block allows you to reverse an array. Once applied, the first item of the array becomes the last, and the last item of the array becomes the first.

In the above solution under Recipe 10-10, initially the array had three elements in the following sequence: a, b, c. After applying the reverse block, the **for element** block is used to traverse through each element and display on the micro:bit LED screen using the **show string** block.

When you run the solution under Recipe 10-10, you will get the following output.

---

c b a

CHAPTER 11

Playing Music

In this chapter, you will learn how to use the Music package of the MakeCode for micro:bit to build and play simple tunes. MakeCode allows you to build music by combining music tones, octaves, beats (duration), accidentals (flats and sharps), and so forth. You can also use the built-in melodies with your applications.

11-1. Connecting a Speaker to Pin 0

Problem

You want to connect a speaker to the micro:bit pin 0.

Solution

Connect the speaker with the micro:bit using alligator (crocodile) clips as explained below.

- Connect one wire to pin0 and the other wire to ground pin. A speaker will work either way around.

- Once completed, your hardware setup should look like that shown in **Figure 11-1**.

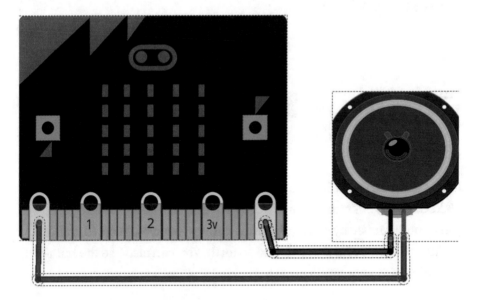

Figure 11-1. *Wiring diagram*

Now create the code as described below and flash it into your micro:bit.

- In the **Toolbox**, click on the **Music** category. Then click
  and drag the **ring tone (Hz)** block over, and place it
  inside the **on start** block (**Figure 11-2**).

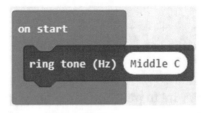

Figure 11-2. *Placing the **ring tone** block inside the **on start** block*

How It Works

By default, MakeCode expects the speaker to be connected through micro:bit's **pin 0** through the edge connector using alligator (crocodile) clips. A speaker has two wires: positive (usually red) and negative (usually black). Some speakers use different color codes for positive and negative leads. With some speakers, you must solder wires to the solder tabs before using them.

Pin 0 is the default pin used to generate music.

11-2. Connecting a Speaker to Other Pins

Problem

You want to connect a speaker to a micro:bit pin1.

Solution

Connect the speaker with the micro:bit using alligator (crocodile) clips as explained below.

- Connect the positive lead of the speaker to the micro:bit pin 1.

- Connect the negative lead of the speaker to the micro:bit pinging.

- Once completed, your hardware setup should look like that shown in **Figure 11-3**.

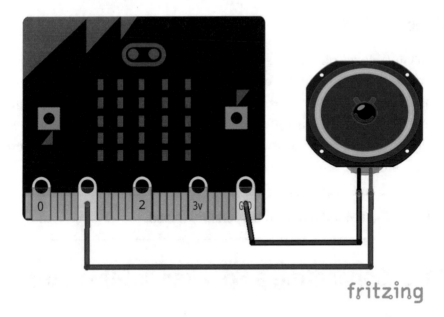

Figure 11-3. *Wiring diagram*

Now create the code as described below and flash it into your micro:bit.

- In the **Toolbox**, click on the **Pins** category. Next, click and drag the **analog set pitch pin** block over, and place it inside the **on start** block. Then select **P1** from the drop-down menu.

- In the **Toolbox**, click on the **Music** category. Then click and drag the **ring tone (Hz)** block over, and place it inside the **on start** block underneath the **analog set pitch pin** block (**Figure 11-4**).

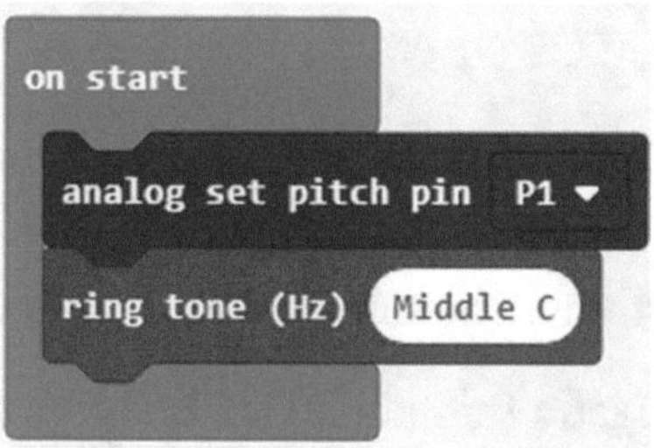

Figure 11-4. *Full code listing*

How It Works

The **analog set pitch pin** block allows you to prepare some pins on the edge connector to output audio signals. Here is the list of pins you can use to connect a speaker.

- P0
- P1
- P2
- P3
- P4
- P10

11-3. Using Earphones

Problem

You want to connect an earphone with the micro:bit to listen to music.

Solution

You can use alligator (crocodile) clips to connect an earphone to the micro:bit without cutting off the jack. **Figure 11-5** shows how you can make the wire connections. The steps below further explain the hack.

- Take two alligator (crocodile) leads (black and red).

- Connect one end of the black alligator lead to the micro:bit **GND** and the other end to the **base** of your earphone jack.

- Connect one end of the red crocodile lead to the micro:bit **pin 0** and the other end to the **tip** of the earphone jack.

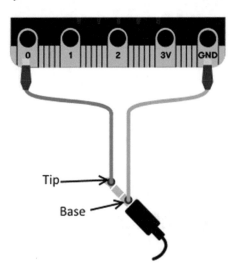

Figure 11-5. *Wiring diagram*

How It Works

If you don't have a speaker, you can still use your micro:bit with earphones. Earphones produce quiet music and are better for testing purposes. If you don't have alligator leads, just cut off the earphone jack and connect the leads to the edge connector (**tip** to **pin 0** and **base** to **GND**) of the micro:bit. However, pre-built audio cables are available to quickly connect earphone or headphones to the micro:bit. You can simply plug the earphone jack to the 3.5 mm socket of the audio cable and connect two crocodile clips to the edge connector of the micro:bit.

11-4. Using Amplifiers
Problem

You want to play tunes loudly with a micro:bit.

Solution

You will need **MonkMakes Speaker for micro:bit** (https://www. monkmakes.com/mb_speaker/) to build this project. **Table 11-1** lists the pin connection between two boards. You can use alligator (crocodile) clips to make connections.

Table 11-1 *Wiring Between MonkMakes Speaker and micro:bit*

Speaker	Micro:bit
IN	Pin 0
3V	3V
GND	GND

Figure 11-6 shows the wiring between the two boards.

Figure 11-6.   Wiring between the MonkMakes speaker module and the micro:bit (Image credits: MonkMakes at https://www. monkmakes.com/mb_speaker/)

How It Works

Some vendors offer speakers with a built-in amplifier to make louder music. MonkMakes (https://www.monkmakes.com/) manufactures a speaker breakout module with a built-in amplifier to produce loud music. It also has a built-in LED to indicate power. The MonkMakes speaker module uses three wires for connectivity and draws additional power from the micro:bit's 3V pin.

11-5. Playing Built-In Melodies
Problem

You want to play a built-in melody.

Solution

- In the *Toolbox*, click on the *Music* category. Next, click and drag the *start melody* block over, and place it inside the *on start* block. Then choose *birthday* from the drop-down menu (**Figure 11-7**).

Figure 11-7. *Full code listing*

How It Works

A **melody** also called a **tune**, **voice**, or **line** is a sequence of single notes that is musically satisfying. The **start melody** block provides you a set of melodies that can be easily integrated with the micro:bit applications. Here is the list:

- dadadadum
- entertainer
- prelude
- ode
- nyan
- ringtone
- funk
- blues

- birthday

- wedding

- funeral

- punchline

- python

- baddy

- chase

- ba ding

- wawawawaa

- jump up

- jump down

- power up

- power down

The behavior of the melody can be changed with **repeating** options:

- **once** - plays the melody in the foreground one time.

- **forever** - plays the melody in the foreground and keeps repeating it.

- **once in background** - plays the melody in the background one time.

- **forever in background** - plays the melody in the background and keeps repeating it.

11-6. Playing a Tone or Note

Problem

You want to play the note **Middle C** when button A is pressed.

Solution

- In the **Toolbox**, click on the **Input** category. Then click on the **on button A pressed** event block.

- In the **Toolbox**, click on the **Music** category. Then click and drag the **ring tone (Hz)** and place it inside the **on button A pressed** event block (**Figure 11-8**).

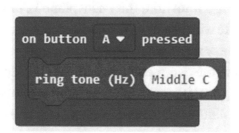

Figure 11-8. *Full code listing*

When you play a note or tone inside the forever block, you will hear crappy sound.

How It Works

The **ring tone (Hz)** block allows you to play a tone of specific frequency. The default frequency of the **ring tone** block is set to **262 Hz** (tone), which is **Middle C** (note). When you click on the parameter box of the ring tone block, a 21-key visual piano keyboard (**Figure 11-9**) will display and allows you to choose a note.

257

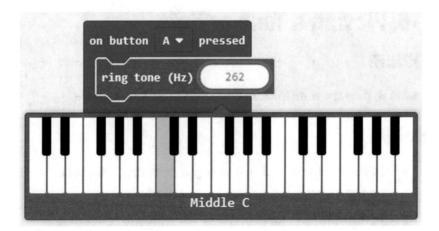

Figure 11-9. *21-key visual piano keyboard*

When you choose a **note** from the visual piano keyboard, the frequency of the note will display in the parameter box of the ring tone (Hz) block. If you know the frequency of the note you want to play, just type the frequency in the parameter box without choosing it from the visual piano keyboard. The precision of the frequency of a note is ± 1 Hz. As an example, for Middle C, the valid frequencies are 261, 262, and 263 Hz (**Figure 11-10**).

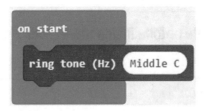

Figure 11-10. *Playing Middle C*

If you type a frequency that does not belongs to a note, the ring tone (Hz) block will recognize it as a tone (**Figure 11-11**).

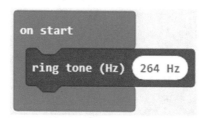

Figure 11-11. *Playing 264 Hz tone*

You can also play tones not belonging to the music notes in human hearable range (20 Hz–20000 Hz). **Figure 11-12** shows the code to play a 15,000 Hz tone for 4 beats. Can you hear?

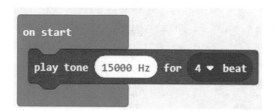

Figure 11-12. *Playing 15000 Hz tone for 4 beat*

All notes are tones but not all tones are notes. In other words, notes are taken from the frequency range (20 Hz to 20 kHz) that humans can hear.

Table 11-2 lists names of all the notes available to choose and their frequencies in Hertz in the 21-key piano keyboard.

Table 11-2. *Notes and Their Frequencies*

Note	Frequency (Hz)
Low C	131
Low C#	139
Low D	147
Low D#	156
Low E	165
Low F	175
Low F#	185
Low G	196
Low G#	208
Low A	220
Low A#	233
Low B	247
Middle C	262
Middle C#	277
Middle D	294
Middle D#	311
Middle E	330
Middle F	349
Middle F#	370
Middle G	392
Middle G#	415

(continued)

Table 11-2. *(continued)*

Note	Frequency (Hz)
Middle A	440
Middle A#	466
Middle B	494
High C	523
High C#	554
High D	587
High D#	622
High E	659
High F	698
High F#	740
High G	784
High G#	831
High A	880
High A#	932
High B	988

In music, sharp (#) means higher in pitch. More specifically, in musical notation, sharp means "higher in pitch by one semitone (half step)." Sharp is the opposite of flat, which is a lowering of pitch. As an example, the Middle C# resides halfway between Middle C (262 Hz) and Middle D (294 Hz).

Musical notes can have flats and sharps known as accidentals. A flat can be written as b (lowercase), and a sharp can be written as # (hash).

Sharps and flats are not the black keys. All black keys are either a sharp or flat, but not all sharps and flats are black keys. Remember, an accidental (a sharp or flat) merely means to play the next higher or lower key on a piano, and that next key may be black or white (**Figure 11-13**).

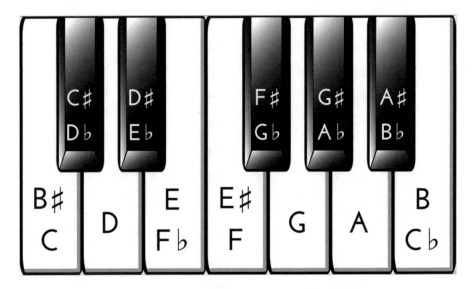

Figure 11-13. *Sharp and flat keys in an octave (Image Credits:* `https://www.key-notes.com/blog/piano-key-chart)`

Figure 11-14 shows how to play sharps and flats using MakeCode. Here are the sound of the notes that you can hear:

- C# - C Sharp

- Ab - A Flat

- Cb - C Flat

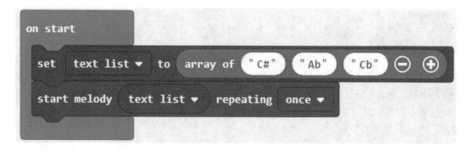

Figure 11-14. *Playing sharps and flats*

11-7. Using Octaves

Problem

You want to play the musical note C in octave 3.

Solution

- In the **Toolbox**, click on the **Arrays** category. Next, click and drag the **set text list to** block over, and place it inside the **on start** block. Then replace each text box with **c**, **c4**, and **c3**, respectively.

- In the **Toolbox**, click on the **Music** category. Then click and drag the **start melody** block over, and place it underneath the **set text list to** block.

- In the ***Toolbox***, click on the ***Variables*** category. Then click and drag the ***text list*** variable over, and place it on the ***melody list*** of the ***start melody*** block (**Figure 11-15**).

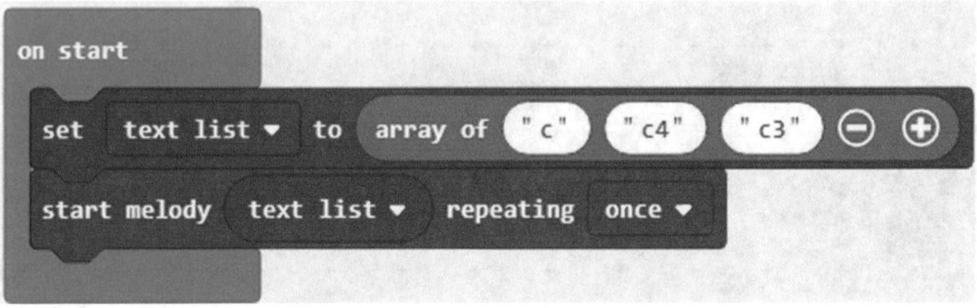

```
on start
    set   text list ▼   to   array of   " c "   " c4 "   " c3 "   ⊖   ⊕
    start melody   text list ▼   repeating   once ▼
```

Figure 11-15. Full code listing

How It Works

In music, an octave or perfect octave is the interval between one musical pitch and another with half or double its frequency. Generally, a piano keyboard consists of keys spanning octaves. **Figure 11-16** shows an octave of a piano keyboard.

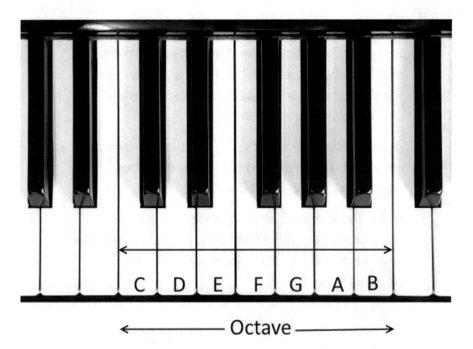

Figure 11-16. An octave on the piano keyboard (Image: Freepik.com)

An octave has seven musical notes (C, D, E, F, G, A, B). A musical note can present with its octave (octave number) to indicate the position of the key on the keyboard. You can write a musical note with its octave as follows.

NOTE[octave]

As an example, the musical note C in octave 3 can be written as C3.

By default, micro:bit plays musical notes in octave 4 unless you explicitly mention it. As an example, the musical note C is equivalent to C4.

11-8. Playing a Note or Tone for Given Duration

Problem

You want to play a note for 4 beats.

Solution

- In the **Toolbox**, click on the **Music** category. Next, click and drag the **play tone for** block over, and place it inside the **on start** block. Then select **4** from the drop-down menu (**Figure 11-17**).

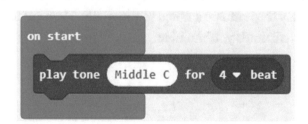

Figure 11-17. Full code listing

How It Works

In music, a beat is the basic unit of time. You can play a musical note or tone for a number of beats. The **play tone for** block offers the following beats.

- 1
- 1/2
- 1/4
- 1/8
- 1/16
- 2
- 4

By default, the ***duration of a beat*** is **500 milliseconds**.

When you run the above code, the **Middle C** will play for **2 seconds**.

The ***duration of a beat*** specifies the arbitrary length of time defined by **tempo**.

Alternatively, you can mention the duration as one of the following.

- Write the musical note followed by a colon followed by the number of beats. **Figure 11-18** shows an example to play three musical notes sequentially. Here are the musical notes you can hear.

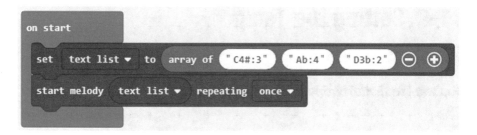

Figure 11-18. *Playing three musical notes sequentially*

- C4#:3 - Plays the note C Sharp in octave 4 for 3 beats. If the duration of a beat is 500 milliseconds, the C4#:3 will play for 1.5 seconds.

- Ab:4 - Plays the note A Flat IN octave 4 for 4 beats. If the duration of a beat is 500 milliseconds, the Ab:4 will play for 2 seconds.

- D3b:2 - Plays the note D Flat in octave 3 for 2 beats. If the duration of a beat is 500 milliseconds, the D3b:2 will play for 1 second.

- Use time as milliseconds instead of beat. **Figure 11-19** shows an example to set 400 milliseconds duration for the musical note Middle C. Originally, the **play tone** block presents the duration in beats with a drop-down box. To type the value 400, first you should replace it with a value box. You can get an **empty value box** from the **Math** category.

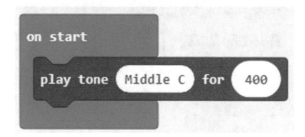

Figure 11-19. *Setting a duration for a musical note*

11-9. Setting the Tempo

Problem

You want to set the tempo to 400 for your music.

Solution

- In the **Toolbox**, click on the **Music** category. Next, click and drag the **set tempo to (bpm)** block over, and place it inside the **on start** block. Then type **400** in the value box. Alternatively, you can use the slider to change the value.

- In the *Toolbox*, click on the *Music* category again. Then click and drag the *play tone for* block over, and place it inside the *on start* block underneath the *set tempo to (bpm)* block (**Figure 11-20**).

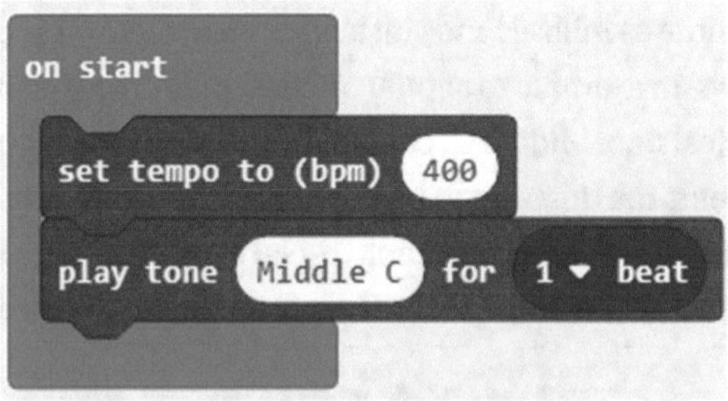

Figure 11-20. *Full code listing*

How It Works

Tempo defines the speed of a piece of music. In your code, the **default amount of the tempo** is **120**. Tempo can be expressed in **bpm** (beats per minute). You can set the tempo for the music using the **set tempo to (bpm)** block. You can type any positive value for the tempo, but MakeCode recommends 4 to 400.

When you change the tempo, the duration of a beat gets changed accordingly. By default, the duration of a beat is 500 milliseconds for the tempo, 120. You can calculate the duration of a beat in milliseconds for a given tempo as follows.

Duration of a beat in milliseconds = 60000 / Tempo (bps)

Example: Calculate the duration of a beat for tempo 120.

= 60,000 milliseconds / 120

= 500 milliseconds

In the above example, first the tempo is set to 400 using the **set tempo to (bpm)** block. Then it plays the **Middle C** for **1 beat** using the **play tone for** block. The duration of the beat is,

= 60,000 milliseconds / 400

= 150 milliseconds

If you want to change the tempo to a different value during the music, use **change tempo by (bpm)** block. **Figure 11-21** shows an example code to change the tempo from **400** to **300**.

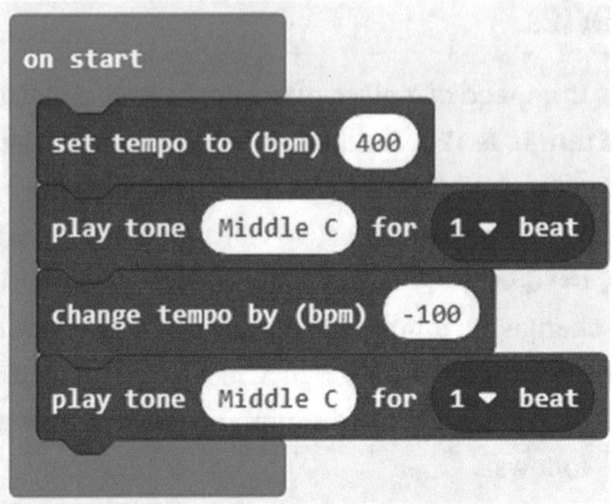

Figure 11-21. *Changing the tempo from 400 to 300*

The larger the tempo value, the faster the notes (tunes) will play.

11-10. Getting the Tempo

Problem

You want to get the current tempo in beats per minute.

Solution

- In the **Toolbox**, click on the **Basic** category. Then click and drag the **show number** block over, and place it inside the **on start** block.

- In the *Toolbox*, click on the *Music* category. Then click and drag the *tempo (bpm)* block over, and place it inside the placeholder of the *show number* block (**Figure 11-22**).

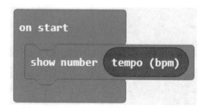

Figure 11-22. Full code listing

How It Works

The **tempo (bpm)** block returns the tempo in beats per minute.

11-11. Getting the Duration of a Beat

Problem

You want to get the duration of a beat in milliseconds.

Solution

- In the **Toolbox**, click on the **Basic** category. Then click and drag the **show number** block over, and place it inside the **on start** block.

- In the *Toolbox*, click on the *Music* category. Then click and drag the *beat* block over, and place it inside the placeholder of the *show number* block (**Figure 11-23**).

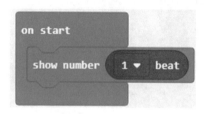

Figure 11-23. Full code listing

271

How It Works

By default, the beat block returns the duration of a beat in milliseconds. It also returns the duration of 1/2, 1/4, 1/8, 1/16, 2, and 4 beats.

11-12. Using Music Events

Problem

You want to display a **happy** icon once the **happy birthday** melody has ended.

Solution

- In the **Toolbox**, click on the **Music** category. Next, click and drag the **start melody** block over, and place it inside the **on start** block. Then choose, **birthday** from the drop-down menu.

- In the **Toolbox**, click on the **Music** category. Next, click and drag the **music on** event block. Then choose **melody ended** from the drop-down menu.

- In the *Toolbox*, click on the *Basic* category. Next, click and drag the *show icon* block over, and place it inside the *music on* block. Then choose *happy* from the drop-down menu (**Figure 11-24**).

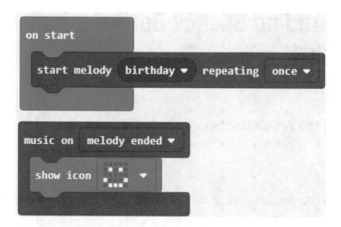

Figure 11-24. *Full code listing*

How It Works

The music on block raises actions for the following musical events.

- melody note played

- melody started

- melody ended

- melody repeated

- background melody note played

- background melody started

- background melody ended

- background melody repeated

- background melody paused

- background melody resumed

11-13. Adding Silence Between Notes and Tones

Problem

You want to add 2 seconds of silence between two notes.

Solution

- In the **Toolbox**, click on the Music category. Then click and drag the **play tone for** block over, and place it inside the **on start** block.

- In the **Toolbox**, click on the **Music** category. Next, click and drag the **reset (ms)** block over, and place it inside the **on start** block underneath the **play tone for** block. Then choose **4** for the beat from the drop-down menu.

- Right-click on the *play tone for* block, and from the shortcut menu, click *Duplicate*. Next, click and drag the duplicated *play tone for* block and place it underneath the *reset (ms)* block. Then select the tone (note) *Middle D* from the visual piano keyboard (**Figure 11-25**).

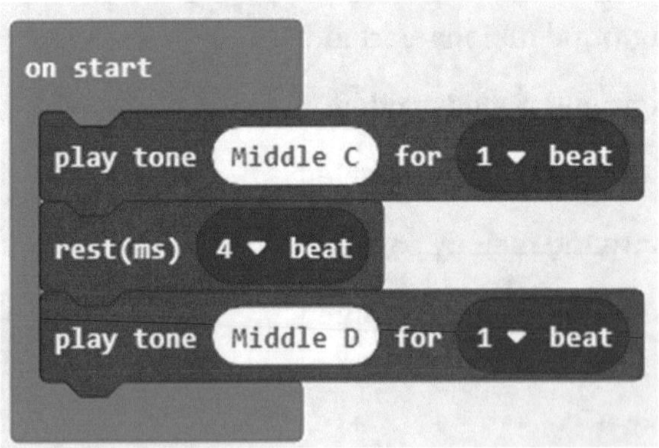

Figure 11-25. *Full code listing*

How It Works

The **reset(ms)** block allows you to add silence between notes, tones, or melodies. The duration of a silence can be in **beats** or **milliseconds**. **Figure 11-26** shows how to use 2000 milliseconds to add a duration for silence.

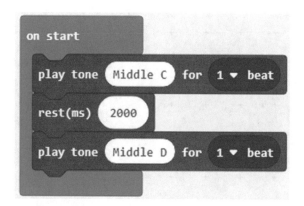

Figure 11-26. *Using 2000 milliseconds to make silence*

CHAPTER 12

Using Sensors

This chapter presents how to use sensors with micro: bit to sense the physical environment. It has some built-in sensors such as accelerometers, compasses, temperatures, lights, and touch. You can use them without attaching any external components to your micro:bit.

12-1. Using Built-In Accelerometer

Problem

You want to get the acceleration values in the left and right direction (x-axis).

Solution

- In the **Toolbox**, click on the **Basic** category. Then click and drag the **show number** block over, and place it inside the **forever** block.

- In the **Toolbox**, click on the **Input** category. Then click and drag the **acceleration (mg)** block over, and place it inside the placeholder of the **show number** block. By default, the **acceleration (mg)** block outputs the acceleration values in the **x**-axis.

© Pradeeka Seneviratne 2019
P. Seneviratne, *BBC micro:bit Recipes*, https://doi.org/10.1007/978-1-4842-4913-0_12

- In the **Toolbox**, click on the **Basic** category. Then click and drag the **pause (ms)** block over, and place it underneath the **show number** block.

- Once completed, your code should look like this (**Figure 12-1**).

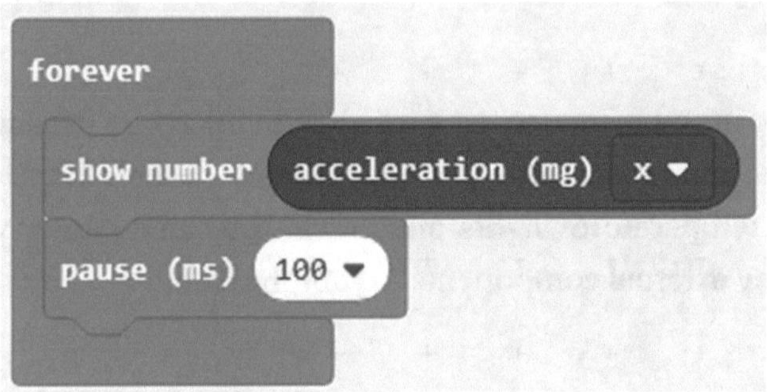

Figure 12-1. *Full code listing*

How It Works

The micro:bit has an on-board three-axis accelerometer chip that can be used to measure the acceleration. The accelerometer is internally connected to the micro:bit's I2C bus. It measures the acceleration or movement along the three axes: x and y axes (the horizontal panes) and the z axes (the vertical pane), which it experiences relative to free fall. This is most commonly called the G-force. With the micro:bit's accelerometer, you will get acceleration values in mG (milliG).

When you place the micro:bit board on the surface of the earth, it will measure acceleration due to the earth's gravity, straight upward of g~9.81 m/s2. The micro:bit accelerometer can measure accelerations between +2g and −2g. This range is suitable to use with a wide range of applications.

The **acceleration (mg)** block outputs the acceleration values in one of three directions (x, y, and z) or as the strength of acceleration from all three directions (dimensions). Following are the options that you can choose to get the output values:

x - Outputs the acceleration values in the x-axis. Put your micro:bit on a level table with the screen pointing up. Initially, x=0, y=0, and z=-1023. Now, tilt your micro:bit board from the left to right or the right to left. Your micro:bit will display values ranging from −1023 to +1023.

y - Outputs the acceleration values in the y-axis. Put your micro:bit on a level table with the screen pointing up. Initially, x=0, y=0, and z=-1023. Now, tilt your micro:bit board forward and backward. Your micro:bit will display values ranging from −1023 to +1023.

z - Outputs the acceleration values in the z-axis. Put your micro:bit on a level table with the screen pointing up. Initially, x=0, y=0, and z=-1023. Now, move your micro:bit up and down. Your micro:bit will display values ranging from −1023 to +1023.

strength - Outputs **combined force** in all directions (x, y, and z) also known as the **overall acceleration**. The overall acceleration can be calculated by the Pythagorean theorem. The formula uses the acceleration along the x, y, and z axes as shown below.

$$acceleration = \sqrt{x^2 + y^2 + z^2}$$

The same formula can be implemented with MakeCode as shown in **Figure 12-2**.

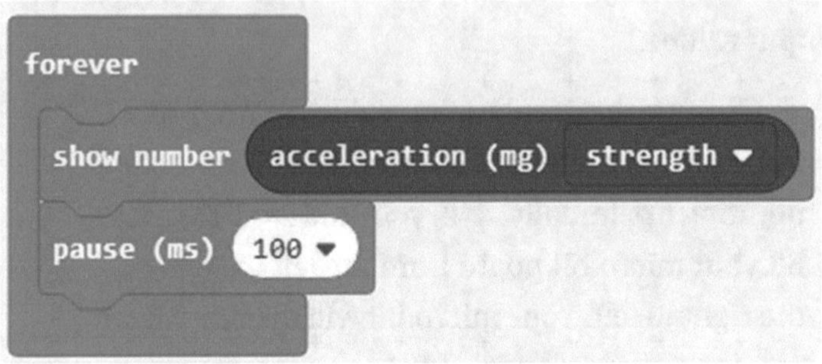

Figure 12-2. *Displaying overall acceleration*

Watch this great video located at https://youtu.be/byngcwj051U to learn how the accelerometer on micro:bit works.

12-2. Using Gestures

Problem

You want to display a random number from 1 to 6, when you shake your micro:bit.

Solution

- In the **Toolbox**, click on the **Input** category and then click on the **on shake** block.

- In the **Toolbox**, click on the **Basic** category. Then click and drag the **show number** block over, and place it inside the **on shake** block.

- In the **Toolbox**, click on the **Math** category. Then click and drag the **pick random** block over, and place it inside the placeholder of the **show number** block.

- In the **pick random** block, type **1** for the **minimum** and **6** for the **maximum** value.

- Once completed, your code should look like that in **Figure 12-3**.

Figure 12-3. *Full code listing*

How It Works

The micro:bit's built-in accelerometer can also be used to create interactive applications based on gestures. In MakeCode, on shake is the default block for gesture detection. If you want to test different gestures, click on the drop-down list and choose one of the following.

- Shake
- Logo up
- Logo down
- Screen up
- Screen down
- Tilt left

- Tilt right

- Free fall

- 3g

- 6g

- 8g

Figure 12-4 shows the graphical representation of each gesture so that you can get an idea about how to make gestures with micro:bit by holding the micro:bit in your hand.

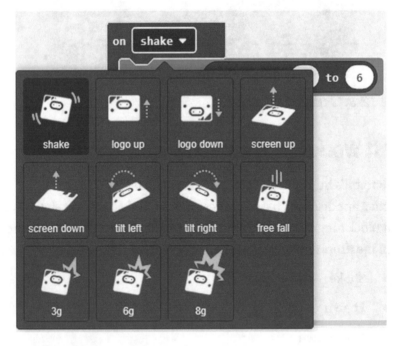

Figure 12-4. Accelerometer gestures

12-3. Using Compass

Problem

You want to find which direction on a compass the micro:bit is facing.

Solution

- In the **Toolbox**, click on the **Variables** category. Next, click on the **Make a Variable** button. In the **New variable name** window, type **degrees**. Then click on the **Ok** button.

- In the **Toolbox**, click on the **Input** category. Then click and drag the **compass heading** block over, and place it inside the *placeholder* of the of the **set degrees to** block.

- In the **Toolbox**, click on the **Logic** category. Next, click and drag the **if-then-else** block over, and place it underneath the **set degrees to** block. Then add more **else if** branches as shown in **Figure 12-5**. Use the **show arrow** block to display different directions.

- The conditional statements for **if**, **else if**, and **else** are as follows:

  - If **degrees < 45**, then show arrow **north**

  - If **degrees < 135**, then show arrow **east**

  - If **degrees < 255**, then show arrow **south**

  - If **degrees < 315,** then show arrow **west**

  - Else, show arrow *north*

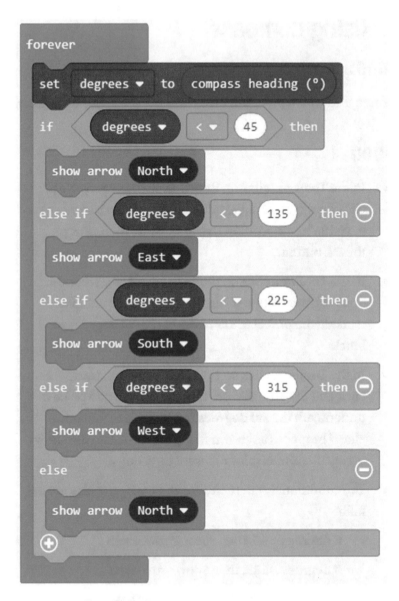

Figure 12-5. *Full code listing*

How It Works

The dedicated magnetometer chip located on the back of your micro:bit measures the compass heading from 0 to 359 degrees. If the compass is not ready, it returns −1003. The micro:bit compass is based on the NXP/Freescale MAG3110, which is a three-axis magnetometer sensor that can be accessed through the I2C bus. The compass can also act as a metal detector.

In the above solution under Recipe 12-3, the following ranges of values are used to find the direction the micro:bit is facing:

- **North**: 315–44 degree

- **East**: 45–134 degrees

- **South**: 135–224 degrees

- **West**: 225–314 degrees

12-4. Calibrating the Compass

Problem

You want to calibrate the built-in compass.

Solution

- In the **Toolbox**, click on the **Input** category. Then click and drag the **calibrate compass** block over, and place it inside the **on start** block (**Figure 12-6**).

Figure 12-6. *Full code listing*

How It Works

Before using the compass, you should calibrate it to ensure correct readings. It is also wise to calibrate the compass each time you use it in a new location.

In some situations, when the compass needs to be calibrated, the micro:bit will automatically prompt the user to calibrate it. However, the calibration sequence can also be manually started with the **calibrate compass** block.

You can place the calibrate compass block at any point in your code, when you need to calibrate the compass. Sometimes the compass may not work even after calibration. It can give spurious results, so it shouldn't be relied on fully for navigation.

12-5. Using Built-In Temperature Sensor

Problem

You want to read the air temperature surrounding your micro:bit in Celsius.

Solution

- In the **Toolbox**, click on the **Basic** category. Then click and drag the **show number** block over, and place it inside the **forever** block.

- In the **Toolbox**, click on the **Input** category. Then click and drag the **temperature** block over, and place it inside the *placeholder* of the **show number** block.

- In the **Toolbox**, click on the **Basic** category. Then click and drag the **pause (ms)** block over, and place it underneath the **show number** block.

- Once completed, your code should look like the following (**Figure 12-7**).

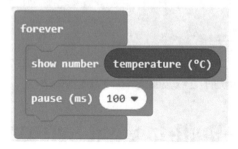

Figure 12-7. *Full code listing*

How It Works

The micro:bit doesn't have a dedicated temperature sensor. Instead, the **temperature** block outputs the temperature of the micro:bit's main CPU. The temperature is a good approximation of the air temperature where your micro:bit is kept and known as **ambient temperature**.

In the above solution under Recipe 12-5, the **temperature** block outputs the CPU temperature in Celsius. The **forever** and the **show number** blocks are used to continually update and display the temperature values on the micro:bit's LED screen.

If you want to display the temperature in **Fahrenheit**, implement the following formula to convert Celsius into Fahrenheit using blocks.

$$\text{Fahrenheit} = ((\text{Celsius} \times 9) / 5) + 32$$

Figure 12-8 shows how to arrange blocks to convert Celsius to Fahrenheit.

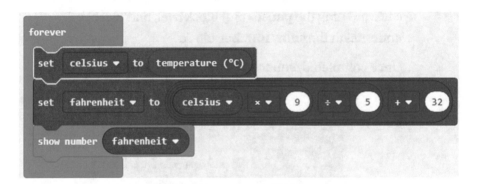

Figure 12-8. *Converting Celsius to Fahrenheit*

12-6. Using Built-In Light Sensor

Problem

You want to find the light level around your micro:bit.

Solution

- In the **Toolbox**, click on the **Variables** category. Next, click on the **Make a Variable** button. In the **New variable name** window, type **reading**. Then click on the **Ok** button.

- In the **Toolbox**, click on the **Input** category. Then click and drag the **light level** block over, and place it inside the *placeholder* of the **set reading to** block.

- In the **Toolbox**, click on the **Led** category. Then click and drag the **plot bar graph of** block over, and place it underneath the **set reading to** block.

- In the **Toolbox**, click on the **Variables** category. Next, click and drag the variable named **reading** over and place it inside the *first placeholder* of the **plot bar graph of** block. Then type **255** in the *second value box*.

- Once completed, your code should look like the following (**Figure 12-9**).

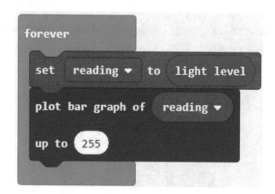

Figure 12-9. *Full code listing*

How It Works

The micro:bit doesn't have a dedicated light sensor. Instead, when you shine light on the front of your micro:bit, it measures the capacitance across a number of LEDs on the front of the board. Then these values are averaged together and give you a number between 0 and 255. The 0 indicates darkness and the 255 indicates bright light. The **plot bar graph** block is used to display a vertical bar graph based on the light level.

12-7. Using Touch Pins

Problem

You want to display the **happy** icon when you touch the pin 0.

Solution

- In the **Toolbox**, click on the **Input** category and then click on the **on pin P0 pressed** block.

- In the **Toolbox**, click on the **Basic** category. Now, click and drag the **show icon** block over, and place it inside the **on pin P0 pressed** block. Then choose the **happy** icon from the drop-down list.

- Once completed, your code should look like that shown in **Figure 12-10**.

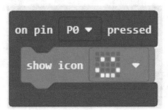

Figure 12-10.   Full code listing

How It Works

Micro:bit board has three specialized pins in the edge connector with large pads, known as touch pins. They are pins 0, 1, and 2. These pins can be used to build touch-sensitive applications based on the analog input. The large connector pads allow you to touch them with your fingertips to change the capacitance of the internal circuit.

CHAPTER 13

Using Bluetooth Services

The micro:bit uses Bluetooth Low Energy, a power-friendly version of Bluetooth technology that allows for wireless communication between smartphones and tablets, allowing for seamless connection to the Internet of things. This chapter presents some of the basic things that you can do with Bluetooth Low Energy.

13-1. Adding Bluetooth Services Extension

Problem

You want to add the Bluetooth Services extension to the MakeCode editor.

Solution

- In the **Toolbox**, click on **Advanced** to expand the package list. Now, scroll down the package list and click on **Extensions**.

- In the **Extensions** page, click on the **bluetooth (Bluetooth services)** (**Figure 13-1**).

© Pradeeka Seneviratne 2019
P. Seneviratne, *BBC micro:bit Recipes*, https://doi.org/10.1007/978-1-4842-4913-0_13

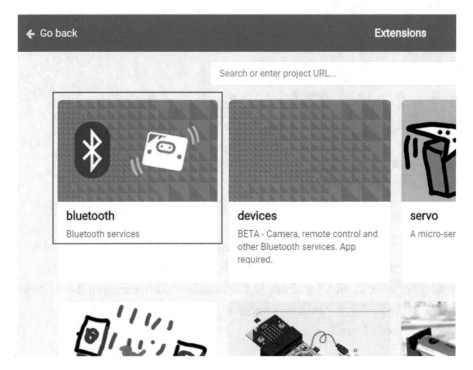

Figure 13-1. *Extensions page*

- In the **Some extensions will be removed** window,
  click **Remove extension(s) and add bluetooth** button
  (**Figure 13-2**).

Figure 13-2. *Confirmation dialog box*

How It Works

Bluetooth extension allows device like a smartphone to use any of the Bluetooth "services" that the micro:bit has. If you want to use the features of the Bluetooth extension, it must first be paired with the micro:bit.

Once enabled, the extension can be found in the Toolbox and ready for access. The Bluetooth extension is incompatible with the radio, radio-broadcast, and NeoPixel extensions. You must first remove these extensions to add the Bluetooth extension.

13-2. Pairing Your micro:bit
Problem

You want to pair your micro:bit with your smartphone or tablet using Bluetooth.

Solution

The following steps guide you on how to pair your micro:bit with a smartphone or tablet running on an Android operating system.

- Go to **Google Play Store** and search for the **BBC micro:bit**. From the search result, choose the official micro:bit app (**Figure 13-3**).

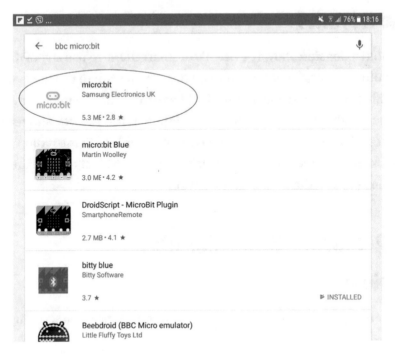

Figure 13-3. *The official micro:bit app*

- Choose **INSTALL** to install the app on your Android smartphone or tablet (**Figure 13-4**).

Figure 13-4. *Installing the micro:bit app*

- After installed, open the app by choosing the **OPEN** button.

- From the micro:bit app, select the **CONNECT** button.

- In the **Connect** page, select the **PAIR A NEW MICRO:BIT** button.

- In **STEP 1**, on the micro:bit, hold down the button **A** and **B** on the front of the board and **reset** button on the back of the board for 3 seconds and then release the **reset** button.

- The micro:bit display will fill up and display the **Bluetooth logo** to indicate that it has entered the pairing mode.

- Select **NEXT** on the Android device, and copy the pattern that is displayed on the micro:bit into the micro:bit app.

- In **STEP 2**, Select **PAIR** on the Android device to search for the micro:bit.

- If the pairing is successful, you will get a message on the screen and a tick on the micro:bit.

- Finally, press the reset button on the micro:bit to complete the pairing process.

The following steps guide you on how to pair your micro:bit with a smartphone or tablet running iOS.

- Go to the **iTunes app store** and search for the **BBC micro:bit**.

- Then install the official micro:bit app; on your iPhone or iPad, Open the app.

- From the micro:bit app, select **Choose micro:bit**.

- In the **Choose micro:bit** page, select **Pair a new micro:bit**.

- On the micro:bit, hold down the button **A** and **B** on the front of the board and **reset** button on the back of the board for 3 seconds and then release the **reset** button.

- The micro:bit display will fill up and display the Bluetooth logo to indicate that it has entered the pairing mode.

- Select **NEXT** on the iOS device, and copy the pattern that is displayed on the micro:bit into the micro:bit app.

- In **STEP 2**, Select **PAIR** on the iOS device to search for the micro:bit.

- If the pairing is successful, you will get a message on the screen and a tick on the micro:bit.

- Finally, press the reset button on the micro:bit to complete the pairing process.

How It Works

The micro:bit app allows you to create code, flash the compiled hex file onto micro:bit hardware, and interface with the device components (e.g., Camera) of a smartphone or tablet.

Connecting your micro:bit to your smartphone or tablet using Bluetooth for the first time is known as pairing. As a prerequisite, you must install an app on your Android or iOS device to pair, connect, and communicate with your micro:bit.

You can download the official micro:bit app for Android, developed by Samsung Electronics, UK, at Google play (https://play.google.com/store/apps/details?id=com.samsung.microbit&hl=en). This will require Android 4.4 or higher installed on your mobile device.

If you have an Apple iPhone or iPad, you can download the micro:bit app from iTunes app store at `https://itunes.apple.com/us/app/micro-bit/id1092687276?mt=8`. The micro:bit app for iOS is currently compatible with a wide range of iPhone and iPad devices with different combinations of hardware components and iOS versions. The list of compatible devices can be found on the app's download page.

13-3. Setting the Transmission Power

Problem

You want to set the transmission power of the Bluetooth module to 3.

Solution

- In the **Toolbox**, click on the **Bluetooth** category. Then click and drag the **bluetooth set transmit power** block over and place it inside the **on start** block.

- Type **3** in the value box (**Figure 13-5**).

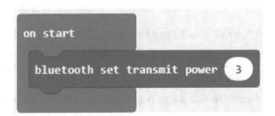

Figure 13-5. *Full code listing*

How It Works

The **bluetooth set transmit power** block allows you to set the transmission power of the Bluetooth radio module on your micro:bit board. You can provide the transmission power as a number in the range **0** to **7**, where **0** is the lowest power and **7** is the highest power. The default power is **7**.

Using high transmit power results in a longer range but requires more battery power.

13-4. Bluetooth Connecting

Problem

You want to display 'connected' or something like that on the screen when your phone (or tablet) gets connected to your micro:bit using Bluetooth.

Solution

- In the **Toolbox**, click on the **Bluetooth** category. Then click on the **on bluetooth connected** event handler block.

- In the **Toolbox**, click on the **Basic** category. Next, click and drag the **show string** block over, and place it inside **on bluetooth connected** block. Then type **Connected** in the textbox (**Figure 13-6**).

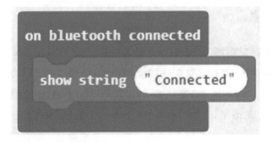

Figure 13-6. *Full code listing*

How It Works

Any code you put inside the **on bluetooth connected** will run when
something connects to your micro:bit using **Bluetooth**. This is very useful
to indicate to users about the status of the Bluetooth connection between
your smartphone (or tablet) and the micro:bit.

13-5. Bluetooth Disconnecting

Problem

You want to display 'Disconnected' or something like that on the screen
when the Bluetooth connection gets disconnected between your phone (or
tablet) and the micro:bit.

Solution

- In the **Toolbox**, click on the **Bluetooth** category. Then
  click on the **on bluetooth disconnected** event handler
  block.

- In the **Toolbox**, click on the **Basic** category. Next,
  click and drag the **show string** block over, and place
  it inside **on bluetooth disconnected** block. Then type
  Disconnected in the textbox (**Figure 13-7**).

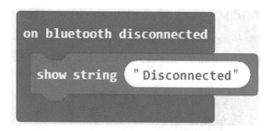

Figure 13-7. *Full code listing*

How It Works

Any code you put inside the **on bluetooth disconnected** will run when the Bluetooth connection disconnects between your phone and the micro:bit. This is very useful to indicate to users about the status of the Bluetooth connection between your smartphone (or tablet) and the micro:bit.

13-6. Using Bluetooth UART to Send String

Problem

- You want to send text from your micro:bit to your Android running smartphone (or tablet) using the Bluetooth UART service.

Solution

This solution assumes that you have already installed **micro:bit UART Terminal app** (https://play.google.com/store/apps/details?id=com.ble.microbit.uart) on your smartphone (or tablet) running **Android** and also paired your micro:bit with the same smartphone (or tablet) using Bluetooth.

- In the **Toolbox**, click on the **Bluetooth** category. Next, click and drag the **bluetooth uart service** block over, and place it inside the **on start** block (**Figure 13-8**).

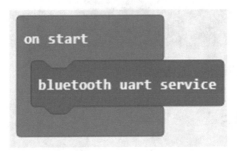

Figure 13-8. *Placing the **bluetooth uart services** block*

- In the **Toolbox**, click on the **Input** category and then click on the **on button A pressed** event block.

- In the **Toolbox**, click on the **Bluetooth** category. Next, click and drag the **bluetooth uart write string** block over, and place it inside the **on button A pressed** block. Then type **Hello** in the text box (**Figure 13-9**).

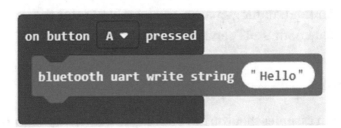

Figure 13-9. *Bluetooth UART writing*

- Connect your micro:bit with the micro:bit UART terminal app by first clicking on the 'double arrow' button, followed by the selecting the micro:bit from the scanned device list (**Figure 13-10**).

Figure 13-10. *Connecting micro:bit with the UART terminal app*

How It Works

The **Bluetooth UART (Universal Asynchronous Receiver/Transmitter) service** allows you to exchange small chunks of data between your micro:bit and the smartphone (or tablet).

The **bluetooth uart write string** block allows micro:bit to send data to a Bluetooth connected device. Sending text involves using the Bluetooth UART service so you must make sure that **bluetooth uart service** has been included in your code, usually inside the **on start** block. In the above solution under Recipe 13-6, when you press the button **A**, the string **Hello** will send to the Bluetooth connected smartphone (or tablet) over UART. The **micro:bit UART terminal app** will show the data chunks coming from the micro:bit (**Figure 13-11**).

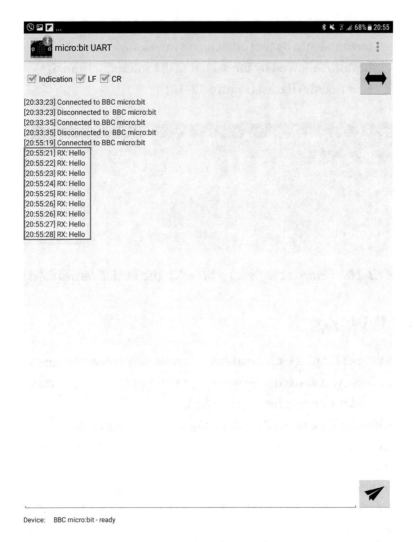

Figure 13-11. *Displaying data chunks on the UART terminal app*

Similarly, you can use the **bluetooth uart write number** block to send numbers to a Bluetooth connected device. You can also use the **bluetooth uart write value** block to send values as a **name-value** pair to a Bluetooth connected device. This is useful when you want to send a set of two linked data items: a name, which is a unique identifier for some item of data; and the value, which is the data that is identified. As an example, the ambient temperature can be sent as shown in **Figure 13-12**.

Figure 13-12. *Sending the ambient temperature*

CHAPTER 14

Using Radio

Micro:bit's CPU (Central Processing Unit) has a built-in 2.4 GHz radio module that allows you to send and receive messages wirelessly for short distances about 70 meters (230 feet) when using the maximum transmission power. With MakeCode for micro:bit, you can build a wide range of applications that can be used to exchange data between micro:bit boards (e.g., broadcasting sensor data).

14-1. Creating Radio Groups
Problem

You want your micro:bit to communicate with other micro:bits.

Solution

- In the **Toolbox**, click on the **Radio** category. Then click and drag the **radio set group** over, and place it inside the **on start** block.

- Type *32* in the value box of the *radio set group* block (**Figure 14-1**).

© Pradeeka Seneviratne 2019
P. Seneviratne, *BBC micro:bit Recipes*, https://doi.org/10.1007/978-1-4842-4913-0_14

Figure 14-1. *Full code listing*

How It Works

The **radio set group** block allows you to connect your micro:bit to a virtual group, allowing it to communicate with other members of the virtual group. This allows multiple micro:bit radio projects to run without interfering with each other.

Your micro:bit can only ever be a member of one group at a time, and any packets sent will only be received by other micro:bits in the same group. You can assign your micro:bit a group number from **0** to **255**. The **default** group number is **0**.

14-2. Setting the Transmission Power

Problem

You want to set the transmission power to **4**.

Solution

- In the **Toolbox**, click on the **Radio** category. Then click and drag the **radio set transmit power** over, and place it inside the **on start** block.

- Type *4* in the value box of the ***radio set transmit power*** block (**Figure 14-2**).

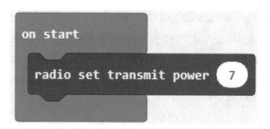

Figure 14-2. *Full code listing*

How It Works

Transmission power of the radio module in the micro:bit indicates the strength of the signal and how far it can go from the source. You can set the transmission power for the micro:bit radio module using the radio set transmit power block. It accepts values from **0** (weak) to **7** (**strong**); the **default** is **6**. The higher the value, the more power the radio module consumes from the micro:bit. However, using a strong signal will help you reach more micro:bit radio modules. But remember, the higher the transmission power, the shorter you can use your micro:bit on battery power.

14-3. Broadcasting String Messages
Problem

You want to broadcast a string (text) message to other micro:bits in the same group.

Solution

You will need two or more micro:bits to get an idea of broadcasting and receiving messages in the same group.

- In the **Toolbox**, click on the **Radio** category. Then click and drag the **radio set group** block over, and place them inside the **on start** block. Same as place the **radio set transmit power** block underneath the **radio set group** block.

- In the **Toolbox**, click on the **Input** category and then click on the **on button A pressed** event.

- In the **Toolbox**, click on the **Radio** category. Next, click and drag the **radio send string** block over, and place inside the **on button A pressed** block. Then type **"Hello!"** In the text box.

- In the **Toolbox**, click on the **Basic** category. Next, click and drag the **show string** block over, and place it inside the **on button A pressed** block underneath the **radio send string** block. Then type **"Sent."** in the text box.

- In the **Toolbox**, click on the Radio category and then click on the **on radio received receivedString** event block.

- In the **Toolbox**, click on the **Basic** category. Next, click and drag the **show string** block over, and place it inside the **on radio received receivedString** block. After that, click on the **Variables** category. Then click and drag the **receivedString** variable block over, and place it inside the text box of the **show string** block.

- In the **Toolbox**, click on the **Basic** category. Next, click and drag the **show string** block over, and place it inside the **on radio received receivedString** block underneath the **show string receivedString** block. After that, click on the **Variables** category. Then click and drag the **received packet** block over, and place it inside the text box of the **show string** block. Finally, choose **serial number** from the drop-down menu of the **received packet** block.

- Once completed, your code should look like the following (**Figure 14-3**).

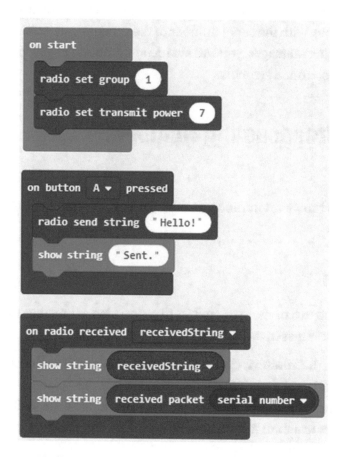

Figure 14-3. *Full code listing*

How It Works

Your micro:bit can both transmit and receive messages. The **radio send string** block accepts any string up to 19 characters. When you broadcast a message, all the micro:bits in the same group can receive the message. If you flashed the above code onto one or more micro:bits, you can send the string message, **Hello!** from one of them to others by pressing the button A. The other micro:bits will receive and immediately display the message along with the serial number of the sender's micro:bit.

With string messages, you can also send numbers (digits), punctuation marks, and common symbols.

14-4. Broadcasting Numbers

Problem

You want to broadcast numbers as messages to other micro:bits in the same group.

Solution

You will need two or more micro:bits to get an idea of broadcasting and receiving messages in the same group.

- In the **Toolbox**, click on the **Radio** category. Then click and drag the **radio set group** block over, and place them inside the **on start** block. Same as place the **radio set transmit power** block underneath the **radio set group** block.

- In the **Toolbox**, click on the **Input** category and then click on the **on button A pressed** event.

- In the **Toolbox**, click on the **Radio** category. Next, click an drag the **radio send number** block over, and place it inside the **on button A pressed** block. Then type **1.5** in the text box.

- In the **Toolbox**, click on the **Basic** category. Next, click and drag the **show string** block over, and place it inside the **on button A pressed** block underneath the **radio send number** block. Then type "**Sent.**" in the text box.

- In the **Toolbox**, click on the **Radio** category and then click on the **on radio received receivedNumber** event block.

- In the **Toolbox**, click on the **Basic** category. Next, click and drag the **show number** block over, and place it inside the **on radio received receivedNumber** block. After that, click on the **Variables** category. Then click and drag the **receivedNumber** variable block over, and place it inside the value box of the **show number** block.

- In the **Toolbox**, click on the **Basic** category. Next, click and drag the **show string** block over, and place it inside the **on radio received receivedNumber** block underneath the **show string receivedNumber** block. After that, click on the **Variables** category. Then click and drag the **received packet** block over, and place it inside the text box of the **show string** block. Finally, choose **serial number** from the drop-down menu of the **received packet** block.

- Once completed, your code should look like the following (**Figure 14-4**).

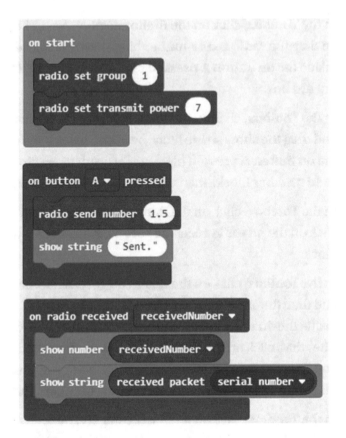

Figure 14-4. *Full code listing*

How It Works

Your micro:bit can both transmit and receive messages. The **radio send number** block accepts any integer and decimal (including negative integers and negative decimal numbers). When you broadcast a message, all the micro:bits in the same group can receive the message. If you flashed the above code onto one or more micro:bits, you can send the number message, **1.5**, from one of them to others by pressing the button A. The other micro:bits will receive and immediately display the message along with the serial number of the sender's micro:bit.

14-5. Broadcasting Message as a Name-Value Pair

Problem

You want to broadcast the ambient temperature of your micro:bit as a labeled message (name-value pair) to other micro:bits in the same group.

Solution

You will need two or more micro:bits to get an idea of broadcasting and receiving messages in the same group.

- In the **Toolbox**, click on the **Radio** category. Then click and drag the **radio set group** block over, and place them inside the **on start** block. Same as place the **radio set transmit power** block underneath the **radio set group** block.

- In the **Toolbox**, click on the **Input** category and then click on the **on button A pressed** event.

- In the **Toolbox**, click on the **Radio** category. Next, click and drag the **radio send value** block over and place inside the **on button A pressed** block. Next, type **temp** in the text box. After that, click on the **Input** category. Then click and drag the **temperature** block over, and place it inside the value box of the **radio send value** block (**Figure 14-5**).

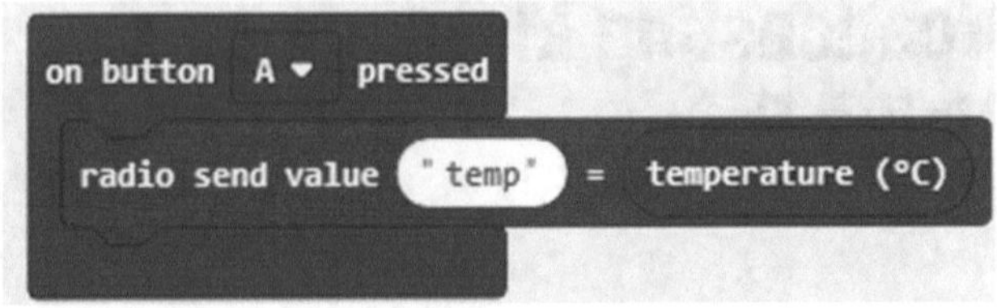

Figure 14-5. *Creating a name-value pair*

- In the **Toolbox**, click on the **Radio** category, and then click on the **on radio received name value** event block.

- In the **Toolbox**, click on the **Basic** category. Next, click and drag the **show string** block over, and place it inside the **on radio received name value** block. After that, click on the **Variables** category. Then click and drag the **name** variable block over, and place it inside the text box of the **show string** block. Same as place a **show number** block and replace its default value with the variable block **value**.

- In the **Toolbox**, click on the **Basic** category. Next, click and drag the **show string** block over and place it inside the **on radio received receivedNumber** block underneath the **show string receivedNumber** block. After that, click on the **Variables** category. Then click and drag the **received packet** block over, and place it inside the text box of the **show string** block. Finally, choose **serial number** from the drop-down menu of the **received packet** block.

- Once completed, your code should look like the following (**Figure 14-6**).

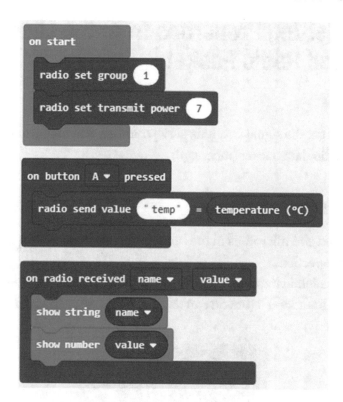

Figure 14-6. *Full code listing*

How It Works

The **radio send value** block allows you to send messages as **name-value** pairs over radio. The name can be anything that can be used to label your value. This is very useful for the receiving party to identify the values with their names.

In the above solution under Recipe 14-5, when you press the button A, micro:bit broadcasts its CPU temperature as a name-value pair over the radio (e.g., name=temp, value=23).

317

14-6. Getting Properties from the Last Received Radio Packet

Problem

You want to get the signal strength, serial number, and time from the last received radio data packet (message).

Solution

You will need two micro:bits in the same group to get an idea of the message properties.

Flash the following code into the micro:bit to work as the sender to continually broadcast 0 (or you can use any number) (**Figure 14-7**).

Figure 14-7. *Sending a number*

The steps below will explain how to build the code for the receiver to get properties from the last received message from the above sender.

- In the **Toolbox**, click on the **Radio** category. Then click on the **on radio received receivedNumber** block.

- In the **Toolbox**, click on the **Basic** category. Then click and drag the **show number** block over, and place it inside the **on radio received receivedNumber** block.

- In the Toolbox, click on the Radio category. Then click and drag the **received packet** block over, and place it inside the placeholder of the **show number** block. By default, the **received packet** block returns the **signal strength** of the sender.

- **Duplicate** the **show number** block twice and place them inside the **on radio received receivedNumber** block. Click on the drop-down menu of the second block and choose **time**. Also, click on the drop-down list of the third block and choose **serial number** (**Figure 14-8**).

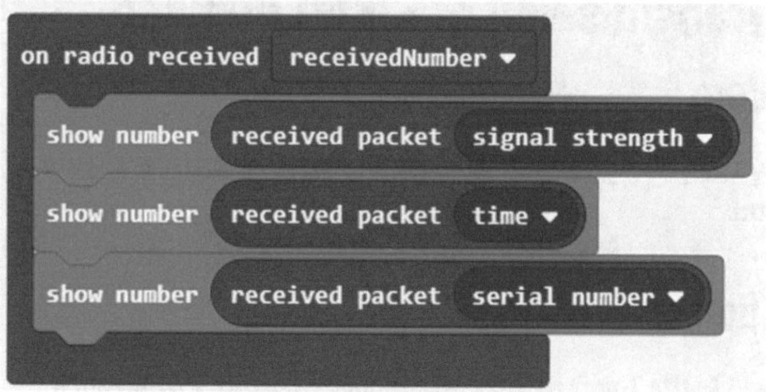

Figure 14-8. *Receiving the number*

How It Works

The **received packet** block allows you to access three properties from the last received message. You can choose one of the following options from the drop-down menu of the **received packet** block.

- **signal strength**: the strength of the radio signal when the packet was received. The value ranges from −128 (weak) to −42 (strong).

- **serial number**: the serial number of the board sending the packet.

- **time**: the time when the packet was sent, which is the system time since power on, in microseconds, of the sender.

When you run the above codes with two micro:bits, the receiver will continually get and display the signal strength, time, and serial number from the sender's message.

14-7. Enabling and Disabling the Transmission of Serial Number

Problem

You want to disable the transmission of the serial number of your micro:bit.

Solution

- In the Toolbox, click on the Radio category. Then click and drag the **radio set transmit serial number** block over, and place it inside the **on start** block.

- Select *false* from the drop-down menu of the *radio set transmit serial number* block (**Figure 14-9**).

Figure 14-9. *Full code listing*

How It Works

The **radio set transmit serial number** block allows you to disable the transmission of the serial number of your micro:bit. When you broadcast a message to a group by disabling the serial number, still other micro:bits can receive your messages, but they cannot identify the serial number of your micro:bit. By default, micro:bit transmits its serial number along with the message unless you choose **false** from the drop-down menu of the **radio set transmit serial number** block.

CHAPTER 15

Building Simple Games

This chapter provides some basic techniques that you can use to develop simple games with the micro:bit LED display and two built-in buttons.

15-1. Creating a Sprite

Problem

You want to create a sprite at (x2,y2) on the micro:bit LED screen.

Solution

- In the **Toolbox**, click on the **Variables** category. Next, click on the **Make a Variable…** button. In the **New variable name** box, type **sprite** for the variable name. Then click the **Ok** button.

- In the **Toolbox**, click on the **Variables** category. Then click and drag the **set sprite to** block over, and place it inside the **on start** block.

- In the **Toolbox**, click on the **Game** category. Then click and drag the **create sprite** block over, and place it inside the placeholder of the **set sprite to** block to replace the 0.

- In the **create sprite at** block, type the value 2 for **x** and type the value **2** for **y**.

- Once completed, your code should look like the following (**Figure 15-1**).

Figure 15-1. *Full code listing*

How It Works

When you build games with micro:bit, the LEDs on the front side of the board will act as the graphical user interface just like the LCD or CRT screen of a video game console. Sprites are the building blocks of a game. You can create sprites, tell them to move and turn, detect whether a sprite has bumped into another sprite, and many more things. Cool!

The LED screen consists of 5 columns and 5 rows, for a total of 25 LEDs. The columns belong to the x-axis and the rows belong to the y-axis, like a Cartesian chart. The address of the LED in the top-left corner can be written as (x0,y0). The address of the LED in the top-right corner can be written as (x4,y0). **Figure 15-2** shows the column and row numbers associated with the LED grid. You can read the column numbers (0 to 5) along the *x*-axis and row numbers (0 to 5) along the *y*-axis.

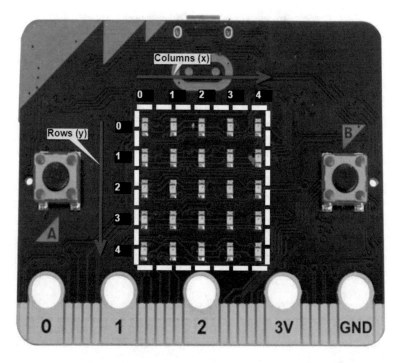

Figure 15-2. *Built-in LED display consists of columns and rows*

The **create sprite** block accepts the x and y positions of the sprite that you want to create:

> x: between 0 and 4

> y: between 0 and 4

When you run the above code, the LED at (x2,y2) will turn on (**Figure 15-3**).

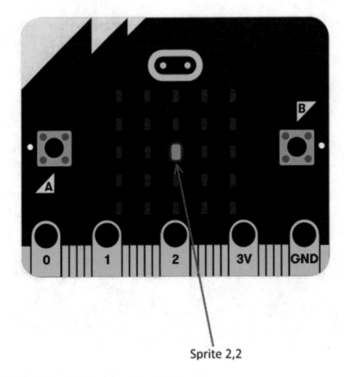

Sprite 2,2

Figure 15-3. *Creating a sprite at x2,y2*

Any number less than 0 or greater than 4 is considered as 0 and 4, respectively. As an example, −1 is considered as 0 and 5 is considered as 4.

15-2. Moving a Sprite Straightly

Problem

You want to move the sprite created in **Recipe 15-1** to the left by 1 LED each time when you press the button A and to the right by 1 LED each time when you press the button B.

Solution

- In the **Toolbox**, click on the **Input** category and then click on the **on button A pressed** event block.

- In the **Toolbox**, click on the **Games** category. Next, click and drag the **move by** block over, and place it inside the **on button A pressed** block. Then type the value **−1** in the value box.

- Duplicate the **on button A pressed** block. Next, choose **B** from the drop-down menu. Then in the **move by** block, type the value **1** in the value box.

- Once completed, your code should look like this (**Figure 15-4**).

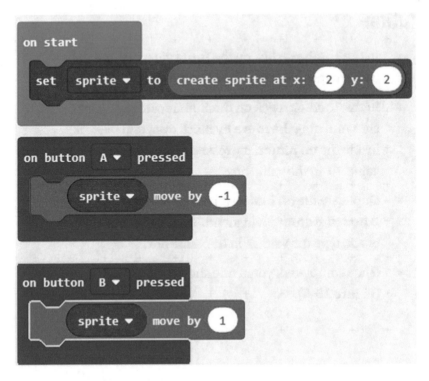

Figure 15-4. *Full code listing*

How It Works

With the **move by** block, you can tell a sprite to move straight on a row from left to right or right to left. In the above example, when you press the button A, the sprite moves to left by 1 LED. When you press the button B, the sprite moves to the right by 1 LED. A negative value tells how many LEDs the sprite should move to the left, and a positive value tells how many LEDs the sprite should move to the right. You can move a sprite straightly to the left, until it reaches to the first column. Similarly, you can move a sprite straightly to the right, until it reaches to the last column.

When you run the above code, you can move the sprite to the left and right by pressing the buttons A and B. **Figure 15-5** shows the left and right boundaries.

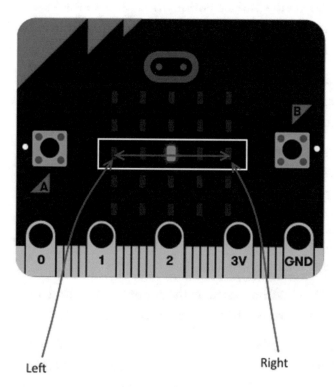

Left   Right

Figure 15-5. *Left and right boundaries for the sprite. The sprite can only move on row 2.*

15-3. Moving a Sprite by Turning

Problem

You want to create a sprite in the middle of the screen. Then move the sprite by turning 45 degrees to the right each time by 1 LED.

Solution

- In the **Toolbox**, click on the **Variables** category. Next, click on the **Make a Variable...** button. In the **New variable name** box, type **sprite** for the variable name. Then click the **Ok** button.

- In the **Toolbox**, click on the **Variables** category. Then click and drag the **set sprite to** block over, and place it inside the **on start** block.

- In the **Toolbox**, click on the **Game** category. Then click and drag the **create sprite** block over, and place it inside the placeholder of the **set sprite to** block to replace the 0.

- In the **create sprite at** block, type the value 2 for **x** and type the value **2** for **y**.

- In the **Toolbox**, click on the **Input** category and then click on the **on button A pressed** event block.

- In the **Toolbox**, click on the **Game** category. Then click and drag the **turn right by 45** block over, and place it inside the **on button A pressed** block.

- In the **Toolbox**, click on the **Game** category. Then click and drag the **move by** block over, and place it underneath the **turn right by 45** block.

- Once completed, your code should look like this (**Figure 15-6**).

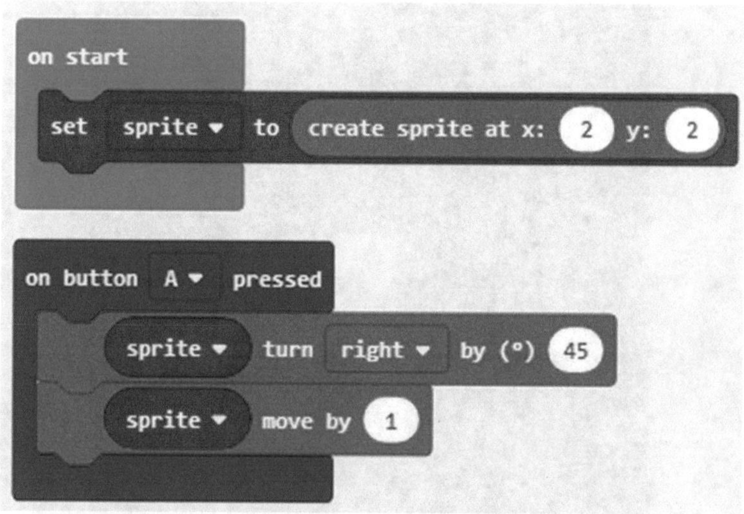

Figure 15-6. *Full code listing*

How It Works

The **turn** block allows your sprite to turn left or right by a number of degrees. **Figure 15-7** and **Figure 15-8** show the path of the sprite, each time when you press the button A.

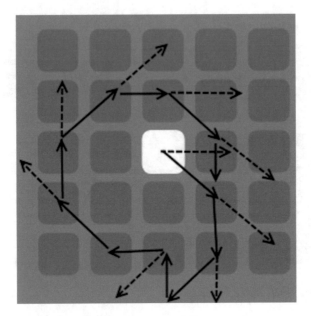

Figure 15-7. *Moving to the right by turning 45 degrees*

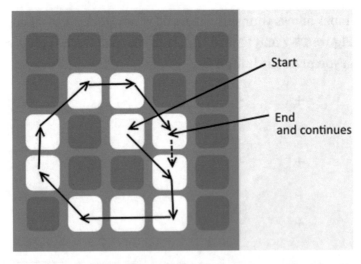

Figure 15-8. *Path from start to end and continues the same path*

15-4. Deleting a Sprite

Problem

You want to delete a sprite.

Solution

This solution assumes that you already have a variable named **sprite** and it holds a sprite (initially at x2,y2).

- In the **Toolbox**, click on the **Input** category and then click on the **on button A pressed** event block.

- In the **Toolbox**, click on the **Game** category. Then click on the **delete** block over, and place it inside the **on button A pressed** block (**Figure 15-9**).

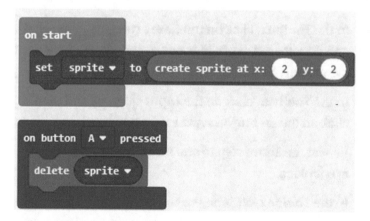

Figure 15-9. *Full code listing*

How It Works

The **delete** block allows you to delete a sprite from the game. If you have more than one sprite in your game, choose the correct variable for the sprite from the drop-down list.

In the above example, when you press the button A, the sprite at x2,y2 will be deleted from the screen.

15-5. Holding and Displaying Score

Problem

You want to increment the score by pressing the button A and displaying the current score by pressing the button B.

Solution

- In the **Toolbox**, click on the **Game** category. Then click and drag the **set score** block over, and place it inside the **on start** block.

- In the **Toolbox**, click on the **Input** category and then click on the **on button A pressed** event block.

- Repeat the above step to add an **on button B pressed** event block.

- In the **Toolbox**, click on the **Game** category. Then click and drag the **change score by** block over, and place it inside the **on button A pressed** block.

- In the **Toolbox**, click on the **Basic** category. Then click and drag the **show number** block over, and place it inside the **on button B pressed** block.

- In the **Toolbox**, click on the **Game** category. Then click and drag the **score** block over, and place it inside the placeholder of the **show number** block.

- Once you have completed these steps, your code should look like this (**Figure 15-10**).

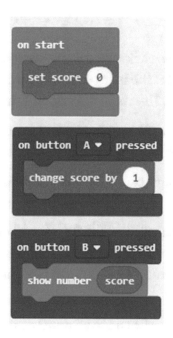

Figure 15-10. *Full code listing*

How It Works

The score of your game can be initialized, updated, and accessed from the following blocks.

- **set score:** sets the score of the game by assigning an initial value.

- **change score**: update the score by a given value.

- **score**: holds the current score.

15-6. Life

Problem

You want to add and remove life from your game.

Solution

- In the **Toolbox**, click on the **Game** category. Next, click and drag the **set life** block over, and place it inside the **on start** block. Then type the value 100 in the value box.

- In the **Toolbox**, click on the **Input** category and then click on the **on button A pressed** event block.

- Repeat the above step to add an event block, **on button B pressed**.

- In the **Toolbox**, click on the **Game** category. Next, click and drag the **add life** block over, and place it inside the **on button A pressed** block. Then type the value 50 in the value box.

- In the **Toolbox**, click on the **Game** category. Next, click and drag the **remove life** block over, and place it inside the **on button B pressed** block. Then type the value 50 in the value box.

- Once completed, your code should look like this (**Figure 15-11**).

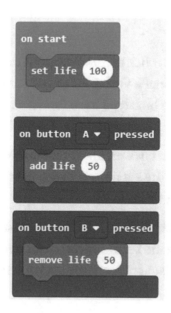

Figure 15-11. *Full code listing*

How It Works

The **set life** block allows you to add life to your game. In the above solution under Recipe 15-6, initially the life is set to 100. The **add life** block is used to add a number of play-turns that a player character has, to the life variable. The remove life block is used to remove a number of play-turns from the life variable. When the life reaches 0, the game will finish and display 'GAME OVER' on the LED screen.

15-7. Hitting with Another Sprite

Problem

Your game has two sprites. One sprite is defined as the enemy, and the other sprite is defined as the hero. You can move the hero by pressing the button A. If the hero hits with the enemy, the game should be over.

Solution

- In the **Toolbox**, click on the **Variables** category. Next, click on the **Make a Variable...** button. In the **New variable name** box, type **hero** for the variable name. Then click the **Ok** button.

- In the **Toolbox**, click on the **Variables** category. Then click and drag the **set hero to** block over, and place it inside the **on start** block.

- In the **Toolbox**, click on the **Game** category. Then click and drag the **create sprite** block over, and place it inside the placeholder of the **set hero to** block to replace the 0.

- In the **create sprite at** block, type the value 0 for **x** and type the value **2** for **y**.

- Repeat the above steps to create another variable named **enemy** and create a sprite at **x2,y2**.

- In the **Toolbox**, click on the Input category and then click on the **on button A pressed** event block.

- In the **Toolbox**, click on the **Game** category. Next, click and drag the **move by** block over, and place it inside the **on button A pressed** block. Then choose the variable **hero** from the drop-down menu.

- In the **Toolbox**, click on the **Logic** category. Next, click and drag the **if-then** block over, and place it underneath the **move by** block.

- In the **Toolbox**, click on the **Game** category. Next, click and drag the **touching** block over, and place it inside the placeholder of the **if-then** block. Then choose the first operand as the **hero** and the second operand as the **enemy**.

- In the **Toolbox**, click on the **Game** category. Then click and drag the **game over** block over, and place it inside the **then** branch of the **if-then** block.

- Once completed, your code should look like this (**Figure 15-12**).

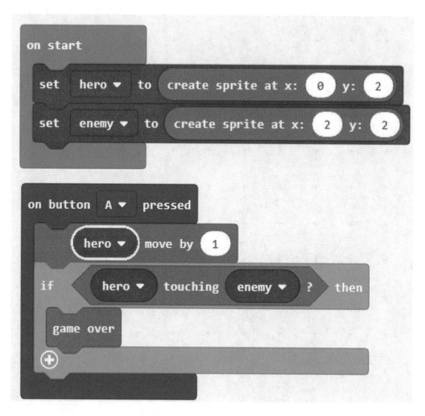

Figure 15-12. *Full code listing*

How It Works

The touching block can be used to detect touching (hitting) of two sprites. The game over block will finish the game.

APPENDIX

ASCII Table

Table A-1 shows all the valid letters, numbers, and punctuation that can be used to build a string. They can be found in the ASCII table from 32–126.

Table A-1. *ASCII Table*

DEC	CHR
32	Space
33	!
34	"
35	#
36	$
37	%
38	&
39	'
40	(
41	)
42	*
43	+

(continued)

© Pradeeka Seneviratne 2019

P. Seneviratne, *BBC micro:bit Recipes*, https://doi.org/10.1007/978-1-4842-4913-0

Table A-1. (*continued*)

DEC	CHR
44	,
45	-
46	.
47	/
48	0
49	1
50	2
51	3
52	4
53	5
54	6
55	7
56	8
57	9
58	:
59	;
60	<
61	=
62	>
63	?
64	@

(*continued*)

Table A-1. (*continued*)

DEC	CHR
65	A
66	B
67	C
68	D
69	E
70	F
71	G
72	H
73	I
74	J
75	K
76	L
77	M
78	N
79	O
80	P
81	Q
82	R
83	S
84	T
85	U

(*continued*)

Table A-1. (*continued*)

DEC	CHR
86	V
87	W
88	X
89	Y
90	Z
91	[
92	\
93	]
94	^
95	_
96	`
97	a
98	b
99	c
100	d
101	e
102	f
103	g
104	h
105	i
106	j

(*continued*)

Table A-1. (*continued*)

DEC	CHR
107	k
108	l
109	m
110	n
111	o
112	p
113	q
114	r
115	s
116	t
117	u
118	v
119	w
120	x
121	y
122	z
123	{
124		
125	}
126	~

Index

A

acceleration (mg)
    block, 277, 279
Accelerometer, 277–280
add value to end block, 234
Alligator, 247, 249, 252, 253
Alligator/Crocodile clips, 117
Ambient temperature, 287
Amplifiers, 253, 254
analog set pitch pin
    block, 250, 251
And operator, 166, 167
Array category, 225
Array functions
    display all items, 242, 244
    index of item, find, 238, 239
    insert an item, 232–234,
        239, 241, 242
    item at specified
        location, 227–229
    number of items, 224–226
    remove, last item, 235–238
    replace item, 229, 231
    reverse items, 244–246
Arrow image, 108–111
arrow image block, 109
ASCII table, 341–345

B

Block categories, 50
Blocks in coding area
    add comment, 54–56
    adding, 47–50
    arrows, 69, 70
    clear screen, 72, 73
    deletion, 51–53
    display numbers, 59–62
    duplication, 53, 54
    icons display, 64–66, 68
    LEDs, 62–64
    pause, execution of
        program, 70–72
    repeated text display, 60, 61
    text display, 56–59
Bluetooth
    disconnected, 300, 301
    micro:bit connection, 299, 300
    transmission power, 298, 299
Bluetooth low energy, 291
Bluetooth services extension
    Extensions page, 291
    MakeCode editor, 291
    smartphone, 293
bluetooth set transmit power
    block, 299

© Pradeeka Seneviratne 2019
P. Seneviratne, *BBC micro:bit Recipes*, https://doi.org/10.1007/978-1-4842-4913-0

Printed in the United States
By Bookmasters